JESUS
AND
EMPIRE

The Kingdom of God
and the New World Disorder

Richard A. Horsley

Fortress Press
Minneapolis

JESUS AND EMPIRE
The Kingdom of God and the New World Disorder

Cover image: Roman aqueduct © Peter Christopher/Masterfile.
Used by permission.
Cover design: Brad Norr Design
Book design: Ann Delgehausen

Library of Congress Cataloging-in-Publication Data
Horsley, Richard A.
    Jesus and empire : the kingdom of God and the new world disorder / Richard A. Horsley.
        p. cm.
Includes bibliographical references and index.
    ISBN 0-8006-3490-X (pbk. : alk. paper)
    1. Kingdom of God. I. Title.
BT94 .H73 2002
232.9'5—dc21   2002013288

The paper used in this publication meets the minimum requirements of American National Standard for Information Sciences—Permanence of Paper for Printed Library Materials, ANSI Z329.48-1984.

Manufactured in the U.S.A.
07   06   05   3   4   5   6   7   8   9   10

JESUS AND EMPIRE

CONTENTS

ACKNOWLEDGMENTS

This book is an expansion of the 2001 Rauschenbusch Lectures at Colgate-Rochester Theological School. Special thanks to former Dean William Herzog for the invitation to deliver those lectures, and to Colgate-Rochester-Crozier Theological faculty and students for their warm reception. I owe much to Bill also for the sensitivity, stimulation, and insight of his books on Jesus. I have been heavily dependent on the research assistance and tutoring of three remarkably thoughtful and critical students: Marlyn Miller, especially on popular movements; Audrey Pitts, especially on Roman imperialism; and Maureen Worth, especially on recent political theory.; I have learned much from Warren Carter on Roman imperialism in relation to the Gospels and Jim Tracy has tutored me in American history. Also, Warren and Jim both generously read all or most of the penultimate draft of *Jesus and Empire*. Most of all I must thank Tom Conry, who worked critically through the first draft and, from his extraordinarily wide-ranging knowledge of the New Testament and political history, offered many helpful suggestions for revision; and Ran Huntsberry, long-time friend and conversation partner, who worked critically through the penultimate draft and helped me see how the presentation might be clearer in important respects. Finally, I continue to appreciate both the many students who have generated stimulating discussions and insights on Jesus and politics and the many colleagues whose work on the historical Jesus has generated new insights, angles, and questions. I may be most indebted to those with whom I may implicitly or explicitly disagree on various issues in the explorations of these chapters.

INTRODUCTION
American Identity and a Depoliticized Jesus

> *Texts are tied to circumstances and to politics large and small, and these require attention and criticism. . . . We cannot deal with the literature of the peripheries without also attending to the literature of the metropolitan centers.*

> —Edward Said

AMERICA'S AMBIGUOUS IDENTITY

Americans have thought of themselves as a biblical people since the first settlements in New England. In leaving England and settling in Plymouth and Boston and Providence, the Pilgrims and Puritans were modeling themselves on the biblical accounts of ancient Israel's exodus from persecution under Pharaoh in Egypt and Israel's covenant with God on Mount Sinai. This formative identity ran so deep that the American Revolution was also understood as a new exodus, an escape from the new pharaoh, George III. None other than the deist Thomas Jefferson proposed that the Great Seal of the United States display Moses leading the Israelites across the Red Sea. Then when the Constitution was being ratified, New England preachers acclaimed it as a new covenant. Just as the twelve tribes had received the covenant on Sinai as a model of civil government and a beacon for subsequent history, so now the thirteen states were forming a new, covenantal model of civil government as a model for other societies.[1]

Although not permitted to learn to read, African American slaves, when they heard the biblical stories of the Israelites' exodus from bondage and the promised land to which God guided them, fantasized

1

escaping from slavery and "goin' over Jordan" to the promised land of freedom. When emancipation of the slaves finally came, it was widely interpreted in terms of the biblical exodus. Again in the civil rights movement, the exodus liberation became a prominent image.[2]

These formative experiences and self-understandings have exerted a powerful influence on the identity of many Americans, perhaps the majority. Sociologist Robert Bellah pointed to the powerful influence of the biblical and Christian heritage on "the American Civil Religion" that frames the religious cohesion of the country, given the "separation of church and state."[3] The martyrdom of President Abraham Lincoln even brought a "Christ figure" into the American "civil religion," broadening the biblical infusion of the civil religion from the Christian New Testament. The more recent assassinations of President John Kennedy and then his brother Robert and civil rights leader Martin Luther King Jr. brought additional Christ figures, along with a new "holy day," into the American identity.

Many reform movements recalling the country to its originary values and ideals (as a biblical people) have drawn on the biblical heritage of the United States. Along with the women's temperance movement and the women's suffrage movement, one of the most important was the social gospel movement of the late nineteenth and early twentieth centuries. Its leading spokesperson, Walter Rauschenbusch, believed that the kingdom of God proclaimed by Jesus had potential to inspire a transformation of American institutions.[4] As he and others preached in the social gospel, the kingdom of God had two complementary sides. On the one hand, the kingdom of God stood in judgment over social sin and oppressive superhuman forces, particularly those of capitalist economic institutions that created increasing injustice. On the other hand, the kingdom could inspire the American people to realize a just political-economic order, to empower the society to transform its economic and political institutions toward a realization of the kingdom of God.

Building upon social change generated by the New Deal, the civil rights movement brought the biblical heritage back into prominence in the public arena. The Christian Right revived yet another brand of the biblical heritage in its struggle to make Americans not just a biblical but a Christian people. Otherwise the biblical strand in the American identity seems to have waned, with some notable exceptions. That books on

Jesus became a bit of a "growth industry" in the 1990s and that network TV as well as PBS and A&E broadcast special documentaries on Jesus suggests that Jesus is alive and well in the general culture, not simply in the churches. Jesus sells—and Jesus helps sell products for the sponsors of such programs.

In another prominent strand of their identity, Americans have understood themselves as a new Rome. In addition to framing the Constitution as a new covenant, the founding "fathers" conceived of themselves as establishing a Republic, in imitation of ancient Rome. They established a Senate as one house of the legislative branch of government. The very arrangement of civic space and the great buildings of the national capital in Washington, D.C., and many a state house bear vivid witness to the shaping of the new American Republic after the model of ancient Rome. In cultivating "republican virtue," the pursuit of the good of the society as a whole, the political leaders of the new nation were eager to avoid the mistakes of the ancient Romans. Ancient democracy had gone awry in the decline of public virtue and the rise of self-interest, as Roman patricians sought their own selfish interests above those of the Republic.[5]

It seems to be a far cry from the originary identity of Americans as a biblical people practicing Roman republican virtue that the United States has recently become the only remaining superpower. After the attack on Pearl Harbor, the United States dramatically ended its long isolation from world affairs by entering and helping win World War II. Then in its drive to protect the heritage of the "Free World" from what was perceived as the imperial designs of Soviet Communism—and to make the world secure for the capitalist system—the United States systematically built what can only, in retrospect, be called its own empire.[6] Americans' reluctance about their empire came out most strongly of course in the movement against the Vietnam War, which seriously divided the country. Nevertheless, President Reagan soon had Americans "standing tall" again, with an unprecedented military buildup and forays into Grenada and Panama.

With the economic collapse of the Soviet Union, many Americans proudly claimed that the United States had "won" the Cold War. America emerged as the only remaining superpower. When the "rogue state," Saddam Hussein's Iraq, challenged American interests in the Middle East, President George Bush (senior) unleashed the U.S. military with its overwhelming technological superiority in Desert Storm. The United States having "won" yet another war, President Bush proclaimed the establishment of a "New World Order," with the U.S. military in the role of the world's policeman. Finally, under another President George (W.) Bush, the U.S. government made dramatic moves to indicate that it would no longer abide by previous international agreements but would act unilaterally. After all, it was the sole superpower.

After September 11, 2001, however (as the cliché goes now), "the world will never be the same." Americans experienced a rude awakening to a new world *disorder*. In addition to our horror and anger at the death of thousands of people, we have been grieving deeply over our losses and we have become deeply anxious about our own vulnerability. Thousands of Americans rushed to help dig out the victims. Millions responded by giving blood for the victims or money for their families. New American heroes were born in the New York policemen and firemen. Most strikingly perhaps was the widespread surge of patriotism: the lavish display of American flags and the surge of civil religious feeling in the singing of the national hymns "America the Beautiful" and "God Bless America." Underlying all of this was the uncomfortable feeling of vulnerability evoked by the terrorist attacks, a feeling that the new world order was also a new world disorder.

Many Americans also began to ask, "Why do they hate us so?" And that led to the painful recognition that not just Arab/Muslim people but many others as well had already been asking a corresponding question: Why do the Americans hate us so? The United States killed hundreds of thousands of civilians in the bombing of Baghdad in Desert Storm. America caused the death of a half million infants and children through the sanctions against Iraq that denied them needed medicines and adequate health care. The United States, an ostensibly Christian country, violates the holy ground of Islam in basing military forces in Saudi Arabia, forces that also prop up the unpopular Saudi regime that oppresses its own people. And, say Muslims and other Arabs, America sides with Israel in oppression of the Palestinians. Before all this, the United States dropped napalm and antipersonnel bombs from the sky on the Vietnamese people, and trained the Latin American militaries that oppressed and often massacred their own peoples.

More generally, the United States consumes a huge percentage of the world's resources, including fossil fuels for SUVs, and then refuses to go along with the Kyoto treaty to slow down global warming that threatens life on the planet. Now global capitalism, which is not identical with but is centered in the United States, effectively controls the economy of nearly every country in the world, to many peoples' detriment. Even if one believes that the power that really controls the world is now global capitalism, it appears that in the twentieth century the United States became the heir of the world empire and now, as the only remaining superpower, indeed stands at the apex of a new world order.

Many Americans, however, are beginning to sense a serious discrepancy between prominent strands in their historical identity and the realities of their current position in the world. The United States would have a hard time convincing the world that it is still practicing republican virtue. Given the United States' behavior in the world, it would be difficult for Americans to claim that they are still a biblical people who hold liberation and covenantal justice as core values and commitments. Indeed, many Americans cannot avoid the awkward feeling that they are now more analogous to imperial Rome than they are to the ancient Middle Eastern people who celebrated their origins in God's liberation from harsh service to a foreign ruler and lived according to the covenantal principles of social-economic justice. Their imperial position in the new world (dis)order may be particularly awkward for Americans reflective about Christian origins. For Jesus of Nazareth carried out his mission precisely among an ancient Middle Eastern people who had been subjected by the Roman Empire.

SEPARATING RELIGION AND DOMESTICATING JESUS

For most, of course, this may pose no problem at all, given the standard pictures of Jesus. After all, in the famous instruction to "render to Caesar what belongs to Caesar" Jesus declared that the empire should be given its due. And in "love your enemies" Jesus is usually understood to have meant that the "Jews" should love, and certainly not resist, the Roman soldiers who were exercising violence against them. The Jesus who defers to empire, however, is rooted in a Jesus who has been reduced to merely a religious figure. Since by definition empire is political, a Jesus who is merely religious has no relevance to or implications for empire. Moreover, the contexts in which Jesus operated, both in ancient Palestine and in the larger Roman Empire, are similarly depoliticized since with Jesus we are dealing only with a figure that stands at the origin of one religion from another, the emergence of Christianity from Judaism.

Since September 11, 2001, however, we can no longer rest comfortably with such domesticated pictures of Jesus. We can no longer ignore the impact of Western imperialism on subordinated peoples and the ways in which peoples whose lives have been invaded sometimes react. The "coincidental" historical analogy is too disquieting, that is, that the Roman Empire had come to control the ancient Middle East, including Galilee and Judea, where Jesus operated. We have come to recognize that the ancient Palestinian people responded to Roman rule in a lengthy series of protests and movements. It is difficult to continue to imagine that Jesus was the only figure unaffected by his people's subjection to the Roman imperial order. If nothing else, then perhaps the fact that he was crucified, a form of execution used by the Romans to intimidate provincial rebels, should lead us to take another look.

A Depoliticized Jesus

We can identify at least four major interrelated factors in this construction of a depoliticized Jesus—most recently in the guise of a wisdom teacher.[7]

1. Most determinative is the modern Western assumption that religion is separate from politics and economics. Western societies have institutionalized this division of reality not only in the separation of church and state and the capitalist economy, but in the academic division of labor. Colleges and universities have separate departments of religion, political science, and economics (etc.). Graduate and professional education proceeds in separate schools of theology, political administration, and business. We then project the modern Western assumption that religion is separate from politics and economics onto ancient societies. Assuming that Jesus is appropriately categorized as a religious figure, we more or less ignore the political-economic aspects and implications of Jesus' preaching and practice.

2. Integrally connected with the assumption of religion as a separate sphere is modern Western individualism. Individualism is a relatively recent and peculiar social development, distinctive to modern Western societies, and especially strong in the United States. Again projecting a modern Western assumption onto ancient society, we think of Jesus as an individual figure independent of the social relations in which he was embedded. And we think of Jesus as having dealt mainly with other individuals, not with social groups and political institutions.

3. Another major factor in the depoliticization of Jesus is the scientific orientation of his scholarly interpreters. Picking up signals from the dominant academic culture, biblical scholars feel constrained to be scientific in their criteria and procedure for investigation and interpretation of Jesus. "Data" from the Gospels must be isolated, analyzed, and brought carefully under *control* in order then to be used in historical reconstruction.[8] Only data that pass the test of modern reasonability/rationality can be used. Having already reduced the Gospels to religious bits and pieces directed to individuals, we then, by scientific screening, exclude the dross of anything miraculous, mythic, or fantastic, leaving the pure nuggets of reified sayings and parables we can test for "authenticity."

The net effect of these three factors is to reduce Jesus to a religious teacher who uttered isolated sayings and parables relevant only to individual persons.

4. Some recent interpreters of Jesus have further depoliticized Jesus by eliminating anything uncomfortably judgmental from the "database" of his "authentic" sayings. They claim that John the Baptist, Jesus' mentor, was an apocalyptic prophet proclaiming judgment, and that Jesus' immediate followers, just after his death, understood Jesus as an apocalyptic figure, the Son of Man, coming in judgment. Jesus himself, they claim, did not preach judgment. Prophetic sayings of condemnation are the later product of Jesus' followers who became resentful about their failure and persecution. Jesus himself was thus not a prophet but rather a wisdom teacher, like the wandering Cynic philosophers in Hellenistic cities, teaching an alternative hippie-like lifestyle to a bunch of rootless nobodies. Whatever the credibility of this picture may be as a historical reconstruction, it portrays a depoliticized individual teacher uttering isolated aphorisms that pertain only to an individual countercultural lifestyle in no particular political-economic context and with no

political implications. It is difficult to understand why the Roman governor, Pontius Pilate, would have bothered to crucify such a figure.

The assumptions and procedures by which such a picture of Jesus is reached, however, are indefensible in historical investigation and reconstruction.

1. It is simply impossible to separate a religious dimension from political-economic life in traditional societies. If Americans were not aware of this before September 11, 2001, they are more fully aware now that in most Middle Eastern countries, it is extremely difficult to separate Muslim faith and practice from political and economic affairs and social life generally. In the United States as well, judging from the outpouring of religiously articulated patriotism after the terrorist attacks, it is difficult to tell where American *civil religion* ends and the U.S. political process and its consumer economy begin.

2. Individualism is a Western ideology, particularly prominent in the United States, but it is largely an operative fiction. Again, as we have recognized after September 11, 2001, if not before, it is impossible to separate individual identity, beliefs, and behavior from the network of relations and institutions in which people are embedded. Identities are always complex and hybrid. People's lives are always embedded in a network of social forms and institutions. As feminist thinkers have insisted, even marital and sexual relations are political. People are always already embedded in complex relations of power.

3. The procedure by which scholars establish a "database" from which they then construct a picture of Jesus is especially problematic as historical method. People do not communicate in isolated sayings. Most communications are far more extensive than individual aphorisms. The meaning of sayings such as proverbs or parables depends completely on the context in which they are uttered and on the cultural tradition in which both the speaker and the hearers are rooted. Rather than purposely isolating Jesus-sayings from the only contexts of meaning to which we still have access, that is, the Gospels, we must start from those literary sources.

4. The claim that Jesus did not preach God's judgment results from application of the dichotomized modern scholarly concepts of "wisdom" and "apocalypticism," concepts that are of questionable applicability to ancient Judean and Galilean literature. Most problematic,

however, is the construction of a historical figure so utterly different from his own mentor before him and his own followers after him.

A Depoliticized Judea and Galilee

Not only do Christian interpreters tend to domesticate Jesus' "ministry," they also tend to depoliticize the immediate Galilean and Judean context in which he operated. Again, we can identify some of the key interrelated factors.

1. The modern Western separation of religion from politics and economics stands at the root of the depoliticization. In modern Western societies, with their separation of church and state, Christianity and Judaism are thought of as "religions." In modern Western Christian understanding, Christianity (a universal and spiritual religion) emerged from and then separated from Judaism (a particularistic ethnic religion). Since Jesus was the key figure in the origin of the one from the other, he is understood as a Jew involved in Judaism whose ministry gave the impetus to the development of Christianity. When Jesus comes into conflict, therefore, it does not have to do with political-economic matters. Rather he comes into conflict with "religious leaders" over basically religious issues: with the Pharisees over the interpretation of the religious law, and with the high priests over the operation of the Temple, understood as (only) a religious institution.

2. Modern individualism is again another key determinative factor. Insofar as Jesus is assumed to be an individual dealing with other individuals, we ignore the fundamental social forms in which personal life was embedded and the social formation he may have presupposed and/or catalyzed. Jesus is even interpreted as having urged his followers to leave their families—the most fundamental social form in any society. Since, in the Christian theological understanding, the church was organized by the apostles after the time of Jesus' ministry, Jesus himself supposedly dealt only with individuals and was not concerned with forming a movement or revitalizing a community.

3. Closely related to the projection of Judaism as a religion onto ancient history, a modern Western essentialism of ethnicity, nationality, and culture determines identity in apolitical terms. All "Jews" are conceived according to the same essentialized culture, viewpoint, and practices. Thus Herod the Great, Caiaphas the high priest, Gamaliel the

Pharisee, and Jesus the Galilean are all conceived of as "Jews," their primary identity as "Jewish." Political differences and interests disappear. Ironically, this depoliticization of Jesus' social context results in generalizations that are highly charged in later historical circumstances, such as that "the Jews" arrested, tried, and clamored for the crucifixion of Jesus.

This Christian theological picture of the immediate context of Jesus' ministry and the assumptions on which it is based, however, do not correspond to the historical realities; indeed, they block our recognition of the historical context in which Jesus worked.

1. At the time of Jesus there was no such thing that could be labeled "Judaism." In recent decades historians of the Jewish people have come to recognize the considerable diversity among ancient "Jewish" groups and views. Accordingly even those still wedded to the concept of "Judaism" have suggested that we must speak of "Judaisms" and perhaps only of "formative Judaism" prior to the emergence in late antiquity of Rabbinic Judaism, which later became normative. Ancient Jewish realities, however, were far more than religious. The most striking example is surely the Temple and its high priesthood. Insofar as tithes and offerings were paid to the Temple and priesthood, the latter were also economic institutions; indeed, they stood at the center of the economy of ancient Palestine. Insofar as the high priests were responsible for collecting the tribute to Rome, they were also politically central to the whole political economy of the Roman province of Judea.

More comprehensively, the immediate context of Jesus' activity must be seen in more standard historical terms. At the time of Jesus, besides numerous cohesive communities of (Greek- or Aramaic-speaking) Jews in various cities of the Roman Empire and Babylonia, there were several Israelite-derived peoples, the Galileans, the Samaritans, and the Judeans, living in Palestine under various rulers appointed by the Romans. Perhaps the most important ruling authority was the Temple and its high priesthood in Jerusalem. But Galilee at the time of Jesus was ruled directly not by the high priests in the Temple, but by Herod's son Antipas. Because of differing local and regional histories, the Judean and Galilean and Samaritan peoples had somewhat different customs and practices while sharing a common Israelite history and cultural tradition. The peoples of Palestine at the time of Jesus appear as a complex society full of political conflict rather than a unitary religion (Judaism).

2. Simply recognizing that the assumption of individualism tends to prevent our posing questions of ancient social forms and social formation suggests that we should at least raise those questions in connection with the context in which Jesus worked. Jesus could not have been dealing with individual persons except in the context of their families and village communities—as influenced by differential cultural customs and traditions and as impacted by their wider relations of domination and exploitation by the various levels of rulers.

3. The essentialism of conceiving the people of ancient Judea and Galilee as "Jews" without further qualification obscures the significant differences between them in social location and historical experience. Some belonged to the high-priestly and Herodian families who enjoyed power and privilege, and were kept in their positions of power, wealth, and privilege by the Romans. The vast majority were economically marginal peasants living in villages. Some of those lived in Judea, which had been ruled by and through the Temple-state in Jerusalem for many centuries, while the Galilean peasants to the north had come under Jerusalem rule only about a century before Jesus. Most significant for adequate historical understanding of the immediate social context of Jesus, modern essentialist concepts such as "the Jews" block recognition of the extreme gulf that existed between rulers and ruled in the ancient world, which gulf has recently been more clearly discerned by classical historians.

A Depoliticized Roman Empire

Interpreters of Jesus also tend to ignore, obscure, or trivialize the broader political situation in which he was operating, the Roman Empire. Examples abound in standard works by biblical interpreters.

1. The story of Jesus' birth (Luke 2:1-20) opens with the statement that "a decree went out from Emperor Augustus that all the world should be registered." In order to comply with the requirement that all should be registered in their original hometown, Joseph makes the long and arduous journey with the expectant Mary from Nazareth to Bethlehem. Biblical interpreters find in Augustus's census a convenient "chronological framework" and "a literary device" to get Mary to Bethlehem, where the messiah is supposed to be born. Even more remarkably, they find that Augustus is serving God's plan in his decree and that the birth of the messiah is thus associated with a famous

Roman emperor whose lengthy reign was widely regarded as an era of peace.

But what about the real purpose of the registration: the Roman requirement that subjected peoples pay a tribute to their conquerors out of their family crops? What about the requirement that Joseph relocate yet again, back to Bethlehem, an agriculturally marginal area where his family had apparently been unable any longer to make a living from the land—hence his implied earlier migration to Galilee (apparently to look for work)?

2. In their attempt to entrap Jesus in his words, the Pharisees and Herodians slyly asked Jesus whether it was lawful to pay tribute to the Roman emperor. Jesus skillfully replied, "Give Caesar the things that are Caesar's, and give God the things that are God's." Christian interpreters have taken this to refer to two separate realms of obligation: to pay taxes to the state on the one hand, and to be faithful to God on the other. This traditional interpretation, however, simply assumes a separation of religion from the political order. But if Jesus' questioners and listeners all assumed such a separation of Caesar and God into utterly separate spheres, then how could the question have possibly been part of a strategy to entrap Jesus?

3. The Roman Empire is standardly presented in many introductions to the New Testament as having facilitated the early Christian mission. The Romans had fortuitously already brought many nations together into one world, which was just waiting for the word of God preached by Paul and others. The Romans had built an extensive network of roads on which such missionaries could travel and maintained the public order in which they could work.

In that imperial world, however, there was already a divine Savior and Lord who had brought "peace and salvation" to humankind and was worshiped with feasts and hymns by those who "had faith" in him. So what were Paul and other apostles doing when they applied such terms to Jesus Christ and the "faith" relationship of believers with their "Savior" and "Lord"? Why were Roman officials regularly arresting Paul and other apostles and keeping them in jail, on the grounds that "they are acting contrary to the decrees of the emperor, saying that there is another king named Jesus" (Acts 17:7)? It seems clear that the Roman Empire was a good deal more than a benign and enabling context for the rise of a supposedly innocuous new religious movement that became Christianity.[9]

INVESTIGATING JESUS AND EMPIRE

While the major problem with the standard interpretation of the historical Jesus is the depoliticization practiced in Western Christian theology and established New Testament studies in general, there are other seriously limiting factors. Most important among these are the failure to investigate, in as precise terms as possible, the particular historical conditions in which Jesus acted, the failure to consider the social form of the relationship between Jesus and those who responded to him, and the failure to investigate in as precise terms as possible the cultural tradition out of which he and his followers operated. If we want to understand the historical Jesus in a fuller and more adequate historical context, then we must obviously devise a more comprehensive and more relational approach (chapter 3).

Working through a more comprehensive relational approach I want to focus on how Jesus responded to the Roman imperial order, or from the point of view of his Galilean and Judean contemporaries, the disorder that Roman imperialism meant for their lives. Once we move beyond the depoliticizing that has reduced Jesus to a relatively innocuous religious teacher, it seems obvious that we must begin with an examination of the practices and effects of Roman imperialism that decisively determined the conditions of life in the historical situation in which he operated (see chapter 1). Trying to understand Jesus' speech and action without knowing how Roman imperialism determined the conditions of life in Galilee and Jerusalem would be like trying to understand Martin Luther King without knowing how slavery, reconstruction, and segregation determined the lives of African Americans in the United States—or, in what may be a better historical analogy, like trying to understand the Iranian revolution without knowing how the U.S. government, by imposing the Shah as dictator, transformed conditions of life in Iran through rapid "development" and "modernization" (i.e., westernization).

Far from being reducible to religion, the immediate Palestinian context of Jesus' mission was highly politicized, filled with periodic popular unrest and protests, movements, and outright revolts against the imperial order that had been imposed by the Romans (see chapter 2). Trying to understand Jesus' mission without a sense of the frequent and intense resistance to the "new world order" among Galileans and Judeans would be like trying to understand a contemporary Islamic renewal movement in the Middle East without a sense of the widespread discontent and a variety of movements, including terrorist organizations. From the survey of the various resistance movements among the Galileans and Judeans we may begin to suspect that Jesus was not a completely unique figure. This survey will make us sensitive to how he may have adapted certain traditional social roles evident in other closely contemporary movements among the Galilean and Judean peasants (see chapter 2).

By common consensus Jesus proclaimed the imminence or presence of the kingdom of God. If we look at the early Gospels as whole stories, and not simply at the sayings, then Jesus was also practicing or implementing the kingdom of God in healings, exorcisms, feedings, and covenantal teachings. Judging from the significance of the phrase "kingdom of God" in the many contexts and connections of Jesus' teaching and practice, it had two broad aspects: the kingdom of God as judgment of rulers and the kingdom of God as the renewal of Israel (the last section of chapter 3). These are two sides of the same coin, two complementary aspects of the same anticipated reality. The kingdom of God is somewhat analogous to the bipartite agenda of recent and current anticolonial (or anti-imperial) movements in which the withdrawal (or defeat) of the colonizing power is the counterpart and condition of the colonized people's restoration to independence and self-determination.

In the judgmental aspect of the kingdom, Jesus as prophet proclaimed God's condemnation of rulers for political-economic oppression of the people. The kingdom as prophetic judgment of rulers had two aspects: condemnation of Rome's client rulers in Palestine, and prophetic teaching that Roman rule was being terminated in the greater struggle in which his exorcisms were local cases of liberation from alien forces (see chapter 4).

The constructive side of the kingdom of God as the renewal of Israel also had two aspects. Jesus as prophet proclaimed and enacted God's renewal of the people in promise of the kingdom's blessings, and in healings and exorcisms of the debilitating effects of Roman imperialism. Finally, in his mission that focused on village communities Jesus proclaimed an alternative social order of cooperation and social justice free of oppression (see chapter 5).

ROMAN IMPERIALISM
The New World Disorder

Without God's aid, so vast an empire could never have been built up.

—Herod Agrippa II (in Josephus)

[The Romans are] the plunderers of the world. . . . If the enemy is rich, they are rapacious, if poor they lust for dominion. Not East, not West has sated them. . . . They rob, butcher, plunder, and call it "empire"; and where they make a desolation, they call it "peace."

—Caledonian chieftain (in Tacitus)

The Romans determined the conditions of life in Galilee where Jesus lived and carried out his mission. In the decades before Jesus was born, Roman armies marched through the area, burning villages, enslaving the able-bodied, and killing the infirm. Roman warlords appointed the young military strongman Herod as "king" and provided him with troops to conquer his subjects. The Roman emperor installed Herod's son Antipas, who had been raised at the imperial court, to rule over Galilee. With the tax revenues he extracted from Galilee, Antipas built two Roman-style cities in Galilee, which previously had neither cities nor a ruler resident in the territory. Roman governors such as Pontius Pilate appointed and deposed the high priests who ruled Judea from their base in the Jerusalem Temple. When the Pharisees and Herodians wanted to trap Jesus into incriminating himself, they asked him whether it was lawful to pay tribute to the Roman emperor. Jesus was executed by order of the Roman governor, and he was killed by crucifixion, a form of execution that the Romans used to intimidate subject peoples by publicly torturing to death their rebel leaders. Even to begin to understand Jesus in historical context, we must have a clearer sense of how Roman imperial practices affected the people of Galilee.

THE EMERGENCE
OF A SINGLE SUPERPOWER
Israel under Empire

By the time of Jesus, the Galilean, Samaritan, and Judean people had lived under the rule of one empire after another for six hundred years, except for one brief interlude of less than a century. According to their cultural traditions, after their God had liberated them from bondage under the pharaoh of Egypt, the Israelites established an independent life in the hill country of Palestine, led by "liberators" (*shophetim*) and "prophets" (*nebi'im*) such as Deborah and Samuel. Faced with the threat of subjection by the Philistines, they developed a popular kingship of their own, headed by the "anointed one" (Hebrew *mashiah*, "messiah") David. Yet the freedom-loving Israelites persistently resisted the efforts of David and his successors to consolidate power in an imperial monarchy.

The Israelites eventually succumbed to domination by a series of empires, beginning with the Assyrians and Babylonians. Indeed, according to the books of Ezra and Nehemiah, the very institutional structure of Judea, in the south of Palestine, as a Temple-state headed by a high priesthood was initially sponsored by the Persian imperial regime. Besides maintaining local elites in power, the Persians encouraged their cultivation of indigenous legal traditions as instruments of imperial policy. In Judea this started the long process by which the books of the Torah (Law) and Prophets were developed into the Temple-state's official version of Israelite tradition.

Ancient Judean literature views the replacement of the Persian Empire by the "western" Hellenistic empires as a severe crisis for the Judean people. To the scribal teachers who received the visions now contained in the book of Daniel, the Hellenistic empire seemed much more vicious than the earlier eastern empires of the Babylonians and Persians. "I saw . . . a fourth beast, terrifying and dreadful and exceedingly strong. It had great iron teeth and was devouring, breaking in pieces, and stamping what was left with its feet. It was different from all the beasts that preceded it" (Dan 7:7). The "Greek" empire expected subject peoples to deliver up the tribute in timely fashion, as had the Babylonian and Persian empires. But the Greeks also pressed their own cultural and political forms on subject peoples. Native aristocracies in particular adopted the Greek language and transformed their societies into city-states patterned after the Greek polis. To indigenous subject peoples it seemed that their aristocratic rulers had abandoned the traditional way of life in their adoption of "western" forms.

In Judea the crisis became acute when the strongest faction among the priestly aristocracy conspired with Antiochus Epiphanes, the Seleucid emperor (in Syria), to transform the Temple-state in Jerusalem into a Greek-style city-state. Led by the priestly Hasmonean family, the Judean people and some scribal teachers mounted the Maccabean Revolt. Although the Hasmonean leaders soon consolidated their own power through a series of treaties and compromises with the imperial regime, the revolt had revived cultural memories and a passion for freedom from imperial rule among the Judean people and scribal teachers (1–2 Maccabees).

The Rise of Rome

In theological schools as well as Sunday schools we learn that in many ways, by establishing order and an elaborate network of roads, the Roman Empire made possible the spread of the Gospel by apostles such as Peter and Paul. But by and large we have little idea of the extent to which Roman imperialism created the conditions from which the mission of Jesus and the Jesus movements arose. Nor do we recognize the extent to which Jesus' actions and program were directed against the Roman imperial order as it had taken shape in Palestine.

The tiny settlement supposedly founded by Romulus and Remus along the banks of the River Tiber gradually expanded its dominance over the rest of Italy. By the end of the third century B.C.E., Rome had become the dominant power in the western Mediterranean by defeating the rival power of Carthage. The Carthaginian general Hannibal had inflicted a humiliating defeat on the Roman armies. Not satisfied to defeat their rival, the Romans took an astounding action that bore ominously on the fate of other peoples that they were to conquer in the future. After goading Carthage into attacking one of their allies, the Romans not only defeated Carthage again, but insisted on annihilating the city in 146 B.C.E.[1]

Concurrent with its dominance in the western Mediterranean, Rome pressed its growing power into the east as well.[2] By mid-second century B.C.E. Roman generals had begun their maneuvers to replace the Macedonian kingdom with Rome's own dominance over the once proud and independent Greek city-states such as Athens, Sparta, and Corinth. After several wars against the Macedonian monarchy and its Greek allies, the Roman patricians provoked war with the Achaean league of cities in 146 B.C.E. (the same year Rome annihilated Carthage). This became Rome's excuse to take control of Greece. Most significantly for ancient Greek history, and surely for the subsequent mission of the apostle Paul, the Roman armies ruthlessly destroyed the great classical city and commercial center of Corinth, enslaved its populace, and despoiled its great works of art and architecture. Rome's subsequent campaigns to assert its dominance across the Aegean in Asia Minor further exhausted Greek peoples, as local economies were drained to support the Roman troops in their periodic expeditions further to the east. In another event of ominous significance for the later Pauline mission, Julius Caesar established a colony on the site of Corinth that the Romans had destroyed a century before. To people the new colony Caesar sent, in addition to army veterans, freed slaves and other unwanted surplus population from the urban mob in Rome that the patrician class was finding it increasingly difficult to manage.

Expansion of the Roman Empire into the Middle East

Rome's intervention in the Middle East contributed to the decline of the Hellenistic empires of the Ptolemies in Egypt and the Seleucids in Syria and Mesopotamia. Indeed, the Romans inflicted a defeat on Antiochus Epiphanes just as he was attempting to quash Judean resistance to westernizing "reforms" and forced the Seleucid regime to pay indemnities. The Romans thus became a decisive factor in the Maccabean forces' success in fighting the Seleucid armies to a standoff.

In a momentous stage of empire building, the Roman warlords finally took decisive military action, on an unprecedented scale, to expand and consolidate Rome's imperium in the east in the early to mid–first century B.C.E.[3] Mithridates, the king in central Asia Minor, had been persistently invading parts of western and northern Asia Minor in which wealthy Roman magnates had already invested heavily. Pirates were plaguing the shipping, upon which the flow of grain and other goods to Rome depended. In a successful climax of a steady escalation in military forces sent to the east, one of the greatest Roman warlords ever, Pompey, drove out Mithridates and "pacified" the pirates.

Pompey's victorious campaigns in the east were a turning point in the vast expansion not only of territory and of peoples controlled by Rome but also of the quantity of goods and wealth flowing to Rome. It was also a significant extension of what Romans understood by their *imperium* and involved an expansion of the Roman elite's propaganda to generate support for their imperialism by appealing to the people's economic self-interest. Romans had recently experienced severe grain shortages. Political orators such as Cicero used the pesky pirates as a symbolic pretext in their patriotic appeals (Cicero, *Leg. Man.* 33, 53, 56; cf. Plutarch, *Pomp.* 24.4–6; Appian, *Mith.* 94). These arrogant and dastardly *latrones* (= bandits/terrorists), who had even attacked Roman fleets, posed a threat to the glory of the empire. *Imperium* therefore was no longer simply a matter of defeating and commanding the obedience of subject peoples and kings. To secure real peace and prosperity, *imperium* now had to include effective control of territory and the shipping by which goods flowed to the imperial metropolis. After all, Cicero told the people (*Leg. Man.* 4–6, 17), it is necessary to protect "your revenues" (*vestra vestigalia*) and "adornments of peace" (a veiled reference to games, public buildings, grain subsidies, and distribution of lands), and "resources for war."[4] After Pompey's victorious campaign against the pirates, Cicero was relieved that "the Roman people" had finally achieved at least the appearance of universal dominion (*Leg. Man.* 56).

Roman leaders of the late Republic thus justified their military and political domination of other peoples by the economic benefits reaped for the populace of the imperial metropolis. The Roman warlords' sustained subjugation of the east marked a new stage in Roman imperialism, and the blatant appeal to the materialistic self-interest of the populace by Cicero and other elite propagandists enunciated a new ("populist"/"democratic") conception of imperialism. No longer content with political domination, Roman ruling circles now deliberately engaged in economic exploitation of the fruits of conquest to supply "peace and prosperity" to the populace of the imperial metropolis.

Such was the propitious international political situation and the domestic attitude when the architects of the Roman Empire finally moved to take effective control of the Middle East. Pompey's march into Syria and Mesopotamia in 64–63 B.C.E. opened yet another key stage in the establishment of Rome's empire. One of the last "corners" of the world to be taken over by Rome was Palestine. As Roman conquests went, Pompey's march into the Galilean and Judean countryside was not particularly destructive. When one of the two factions of Hasmoneans offered resistance, however, the Roman troops besieged Jerusalem and its fortress-temple. Following the capture of the city, Pompey himself then penetrated the holy place of the Temple where none but the high priest himself was allowed to enter. Pompey "freed" most of the cities of Palestine from Hasmonean control, yet he restored Hyrcanus, one of the two rival Hasmoneans, to the high priesthood, and laid the remaining country subject to Jerusalem rule under tribute (Josephus, *War* 1.136–54). With its conquest of the Middle East, Syria, and Palestine, Rome was now the only remaining superpower in the Mediterranean. Although the Parthian Empire still dominated farther east, Rome now controlled the whole Mediterranean world, from the pillars of Hercules to the Middle East.

Not long after establishing its dominance as the only remaining superpower in the Mediterranean world, however, the Roman warlords fell into a civil war that eventually engulfed the rest of the empire, including Judea and Galilee. After an exhausting decade of destruction and death, Julius Caesar's adopted son Octavian, symbolically representing the sober, disciplined rationality of the "West" over the supposedly decadent and indulgent "East," eventually emerged victorious at the battle of Actium (northwest Greece). Acclaimed throughout the empire as the "Savior" who had brought "Peace" to the whole world, Octavian took the name "Augustus" ("Revered/Highly Honored") and "restored the Republic." In the process he also established his own effective rule as emperor.

In extending its imperial rule over the whole Mediterranean world and its systematic exploitation of subject peoples and in Augustus's final "pacification" of the whole world, Rome had thus established a "new world order," with itself as the only remaining superpower.

ROMAN IMPERIALISM

When Octavian finally defeated Anthony at Actium in 31 B.C.E., the elite of the empire breathed a collective sigh of relief. After a chaotic and destructive decade of civil war, such people welcomed the new Roman imperial order that enabled them once more to enjoy their positions of wealth and privilege in stable circumstances. But what about the vast majority of peoples who were now subject to the Roman imperial order?

Because of the modern Western idealization of "the glory of Rome," and separation of religion and politics, biblical interpreters have generally not inquired into the ways by which the Roman imperial order was established and maintained. Indeed, only very recently have classical historians broadened our understanding of the attitudes, policies, and practices by which the Pax Romana was engineered. The more critical recent investigations of the principal policies and practices of Roman imperialism suggest that what was a "new world order" for those of power and privilege was experienced as a disruptive, disorienting, or even devastating new world *disorder* for many of the subject peoples.[5] The brief review that follows concentrates on illustrations from or relevant to Judea and Galilee, since that is where Jesus and his movement were located in Roman imperial geopolitics.

"Orientalism" and "Globalization"

Roman imperial practices were rooted in the elite's stereotyped view of foreign peoples.[6] Even though they admired their culture, the Romans viewed even the Greeks as devious and slavish. They also inherited the Greeks' view of "Orientals" as wealthy and luxurious but decadent, cowardly, and enslaved to despotic kings, in contrast to their own liberty and ostensibly democratic institutions. Just as the Greeks had been fascinated by the Persians, so the Roman elite were intrigued, for example, by the Parthians along the eastern frontier. Latin as well as Greek writers, deriding the Parthian dress in loose flowing clothes, looked down on them as polygamous, promiscuous, shameless, and untrustworthy (Horace, *Carm.* 4.14.41–43; 4.15.1; Trogus, 40.3.1; 41.2.4; 41.3.2–3; Lucan 8.397–401; Strabo 2.9.1). Romans had an unusually jaundiced view of Syrians and Judeans in particular as good for nothing but slavery ("born slaves," e.g., Cicero, *Leg. Man.* 10; Livy 35, 49, 8; 36, 17, 5). They also despised Jews as superstitious and exclusive.

Correspondingly, the Romans thought it especially important to conquer unknown and exotic peoples, "enemies" who were far off and strange, including Middle Eastern peoples such as Arabs, Syrians, and Judeans. The Romans also had a penchant for public display of lists of peoples they had subjected, particularly in remote regions such as Ethiopia, Arabia, and India. The "Accomplishments of the Divine Augustus" that the emperor ordered inscribed on monuments in most cities of the empire includes a lengthy list of peoples subjugated, hostages taken, and regions explored for the first time, including the most remote regions of the inhabited world, such as Arabia and India (*Res Gestae* 26–33).[7]

The subjugation of "oriental" peoples, moreover, was central to the Romans' establishment of their global domination. Roman warlords proudly articulated on innumerable public monuments that they were establishing a worldwide empire. In an inscription on the temple of Minerva in Rome, Pompey boasted that, besides having received over 12,000,000 subjects in surrender and over 1,500 towns and forts in *fides*, he had "subjected the lands from Maeotis to the Red Sea" (Pliny, *Nat. Hist.* 7.96–98). Rome's subjection of the whole world, the *orbis terrarum*, was frequently symbolized by the image of the globe, which even began to appear on coins in the late Republic.[8] "Globalization" constituted one of the principal messages of "The Accomplishments of the Divine Augustus, by which he subjected the world to the rule of the Roman people." It concluded with the claim that he had "made the boundaries of the empire equal to the boundaries of the earth, and safeguarded the revenues of the Romans and increased some of them" (Diododorus Siculus 40.4). As that last phrase suggests, imperial political-military power also meant economic subjection for the conquered peoples.

Emperor Cult and Patronage Pyramids

Although the Romans established their empire by systematic military conquests, they did not maintain military forces in most of the areas they controlled. The Romans deployed no troops at all in the already "urbanized" and "civilized" areas of Italy, Greece, and Asia Minor. Only along the frontiers did the imperial regime post legions on a regular basis, and there the legions functioned not so much as an occupying army but more as a deterrent force, ready to strike against unrest or revolt. Moreover, in dramatic contrast with other historical empires (e.g., the Austro-Hungarian, with its infamous sitting army of clerks, along with its standing army of soldiers, kneeling army of priests, and creeping army of informers), the Roman imperial regime did not build up a large imperial bureaucracy. The necessary affairs of empire were run mainly by the slaves of the *familia Caesaris*, the "household of Caesar."[9] Explaining the remarkable coherence and stability of the empire involves a complex and subtle set of interrelated factors, especially a remarkable interplay of religion and economics in the network of imperial power relations: the cult of the emperor in nearly every major city and province and the extensive pyramids of patronage relations.

As noted above, both the Roman people and the more "urbanized" among the subject peoples were greatly relieved and deeply grateful when Octavian put an end to more than a decade of exhausting empirewide civil war between rival warlords. Octavian, having taken the honorific new name Augustus, was acclaimed as the *Savior* of the world, who had established *peace and prosperity*, fulfilling the hopes and longings of all humankind. Within a remarkably short period of time cities throughout the empire, but particularly the Greek cities, developed elaborate multifaceted "honors" to the emperor Augustus.[10] Statues of the emperor were erected beside those of the traditional gods in many of their temples. Shrines to the emperor were placed at intermediate points between the temples in city centers, and temples were erected to Augustus at the most prominent points in those city centers. Eventually some cities, such as the great metropolis Ephesus, where Paul spent three years in his mission, completely reconstructed their city centers with public space oriented specifically to the temples dedicated to the emperor. The presence of the emperor thus came to pervade public space in the cities of the empire.

Greek cities and leagues of cities also competed for which would give Caesar the greatest honors, creating semiannual games and combination athletic-cultural festivals, with great sacrifices to the emperor. Such festivals involved the entire population of these cities—the only occasions on which most of the people ever ate meat, which was freely distributed. Cities erected monuments with inscriptions that articulated the creed of the burgeoning emperor cult. An inscription from the Provincial Assembly of Asia (western Asia Minor) dated 9 B.C.E. (the first epigraph to this chapter) provides a vivid expression of the divine honors and worship devoted to the emperor as the savior who had brought peace and fulfillment:

> The most divine Caesar . . . we should consider equal to the Beginning of all things . . . ; for when everything was falling [into disorder] and tending toward dissolution, he restored it once more and gave to the whole world a new aura; Caesar . . . the common good Fortune of all. . . . The beginning of life and vitality. . . . All the cities unanimously adopt the birthday of the divine Caesar as the new beginning of the year. . . . Whereas Providence, which has regulated our whole existence . . . has brought our life to the climax of perfection in giving to us [the emperor] Augustus, whom it [Providence] filled with strength for the welfare of

men, and who being sent to us and our descendants as Savior, has put an
end to war and has set all things in order; and [whereas,] having become
[god] manifest (*phaneis*), Caesar has fulfilled all the hopes of earlier times
. . . in surpassing all the benefactors who preceded him . . . , and whereas,
finally, the birthday of the god [Augustus] has been for the whole world
the beginning of good news (*euangelion*) concerning him [therefore let a
new era begin from his birth]. (*OGIS* 2.#458)

These lavish honors to the emperor, which established the presence
of the emperor in ways that pervaded public space and involved whole
urban populations in public festivals and even reorganized the annual
calendar and rhythm of public life, obviously involved huge outlays of
economic resources. Not surprisingly, all these new institutions of honors to and worship of the emperor were sponsored by the wealthy magnates of the Greek cities, the largest landowners and most prominent
local politicians. They had networks of local clients dependent on them,
whether merchants, urban artisans, or rural sharecroppers. They sought
favors from the emperor or members of the imperial family, becoming
themselves clients of the emperor, and thus secured their own dominant
position locally in the bargain. In gratitude to their local benefactors
who funded new temples to the emperor or underwrote the expenses of
the Imperial Games, city councils honored these magnates with public
inscriptions and the most prestigious city offices. These were the men
who held the highly prestigious positions of the imperial priesthoods
city by city.[11] The results were pyramids of economic power and de-
pendencies extending from the emperor at the top down into each city
of the empire.

"Bread and Circus"

Not only did the goods of empire flow into the imperial and regional
elite through the pyramids of patronage, they also came flowing into the
imperial metropolis for the benefit of the general populace there. The
Roman warlords, emperors, and other patricians became obscenely
wealthy. Not only did they bring boundless booty back from their conquests, they also built up vast personal empires of wealth from the
practices of imperialism that made them wealthy and powerful while
impoverishing and ruining the Roman citizen-soldiers. The wealth and
power of the Roman imperial elite was based more in land than in trade

and industry. Vast numbers of Italian peasants who were away from their farms for prolonged periods of time while fighting in the legions headed by the warlords fell deeply into debt. Their creditors among the patrician elite foreclosed on the loans, gradually coming to own extensive estates in the countryside. Instead of keeping the former peasants on the land as sharecroppers, however, they imported tens of thousands of slaves taken in the wars of conquest to work the land. Thus displaced from the land by those they had helped enslave, a million or more Italians from the countryside crowded into Rome and other cities.

The expansion of Rome to over a million—a huge population for an ancient city—compounded the flow of resources from conquered peoples and provinces to the imperial metropolis. In the interests of public order (and preserving their own positions of honor, privilege, and power) the emperors and Roman elite had to provide the populace with adequate food, along with public entertainment—the "bread and circus" made famous by the satirist Juvenal (*Sat.* 10.77–81).[12] At the most fundamental level, the imperial system had to supply the urban masses of Rome (and other metropolises) with food. Under Augustus, for example, grain was doled out to an estimated 250,000 male citizens, affecting (if not completely feeding) around 670,000 people (not counting the 30 percent of the population who were slaves and the resident aliens). The total wheat imports just to Rome itself were between 200,000 and 400,000 tons annually. The bulk of the grain (and other food) imported to Rome was extracted from subject peoples, disproportionately North Africa and Egypt, in the form of tribute and taxes in kind. Herod Agrippa II, with a bit of rhetorical exaggeration, reminds the rebellious mob in Jerusalem in 66 that the peoples of Africa, "besides their annual produce, which feeds the populace of Rome for eight months of the year, pay tribute of all kinds [over and above that], and ungrudgingly devote their contributions to the service of the empire" (Josephus, *War* 2.383). In addition, the burden for such tax and tribute support of the army fell on subject peoples in the frontier areas where most of the army was stationed.

———

The aspects of Roman imperialism covered so far have focused on the imperial metropolis itself and the parts of the empire that already shared much the same urbanized political-economic structure and cultural orientation. To understand how the Roman imperial order worked in the rest of the empire, including the less "civilized" subject peoples of the Middle East, we must explore other dimensions of Roman imperialism. The more we move into the less "civilized" areas of the empire, the more we find that what was imperial *order* for the imperial metropolis and the urbanized peoples, especially the wealthy elites, meant disruption and *disorder* for more recently subjected peoples.

The Glory of Victory

The less "civilized" areas of the empire were controlled by military violence. The Romans glorified conquest and victory. The highest aim and honor for the warlord or emperor was the celebration of a *triumph* in Rome itself at the victorious consummation of a devastating conquest of a subject people. In a highly elaborate ceremonial parade with all the trappings of a grand civil-religious festival, the victorious general led a procession that displayed not only the rich spoils of war but also lavishly constructed floats portraying the military might of the victors and the humiliating defeat of the vanquished. The finest specimens of the enemy army were paraded by in chains, particularly the enemy general or king, who was then ceremonially executed, in accordance with Roman ancestral custom. The glory of conquest was ubiquitous in literature, art, coins, epigraphy, and especially public monuments. Over three hundred triumphal arches survive or are known from coins and inscriptions; and "ritual paraphernalia of conquest," such as trophies, public funerals, and triumphal statues with appropriate inscriptions, figured noticeably in public life. "Victory" was personified prominently on Roman coins. Augustan-era poetry sings the praises of imperial victories, while art of the period provided the dramatic visual representation.[13]

The importance of the great Roman victory over the stubbornly resistant Judean people in particular is dramatically evident in the Arch of Titus (one of the most important tourist sites in Rome both then and now), and in the full description offered by the Judean historian Josephus. The latter also illustrates the inseparability of the Roman imperial religion from its celebration of victorious imperial violence.

> The magnificence of the spectacle . . . displayed the majesty of the Roman empire. They carried images of [the Roman gods] . . . [and led] the mob of captives. . . . Moving stages three or four stories high . . . afforded vivid pictures of [the war's] episodes: a prosperous countryside devastated,

whole battalions of the enemy slaughtered, others led into captivity, walls demolished by engines, strong fortresses overpowered, . . . an area deluged with blood, . . . houses pulled down on their owners' heads, . . . a country in flames on every side. For to such sufferings were the Judeans destined when they plunged into the war. . . . The spoils were borne in promiscuous heaps, most conspicuously those captured in the Jerusalem temple [long list] . . . and lastly a copy of the law of the Judeans. . . . After the announcement that Simon [the enemy general] was executed and the shouts of universal applause which greeted it, the princes [Vespasian and his son Titus] began the sacrifices, with the customary prayers. (*War* 7.132–55)

Terror and Vengeance

Such ceremonial glorification of great victories over subjugated peoples reflected precisely what the Roman armies practiced in the provinces. The ancient Romans believed that to ensure their own national security they had to conquer other peoples with their superior military force in order to extract *fides/pistis* = "loyalty" (i.e., submission and deference) from the subjected people. They believed that any sign of weakness on Rome's part, such as a failure to avenge a defeat in war or to punish a revolt with sufficiently ferocious violence, would be an invitation to disaster.

The initial Roman conquest of new peoples often entailed devastation of the countryside, burning of villages, pillage of towns, and slaughter and enslavement of the populace. The Romans then reacted with brutal reconquest and often outright genocide even to minor breaches of treaty and other threats to the international order they had imposed, all the while insisting that their concern was really for their own security. After viewing the horrific scene of human and animal corpses littering a city destroyed by the Romans, the historian Polybius wrote: "It seems to me that they do this for the sake of terror" (10.15–17; similarly, Julius Caesar, *Bell Gall.* 4.19; Cassius Dio 68.6.1–2; Pliny, *Ep.* 2.7.2). Deterrence by terrorism was practiced by Roman warlords and emperors throughout their imperial domination: "It was traditional; it was the Roman way."[14]

There is no way we can understand such practices as crucifixion, mass slaughter and enslavement, massacres of whole towns and annihilation of whole peoples, other than as purposeful attempts to terrorize subjected peoples. Of the scores of possible examples, we can focus on a few of the many in Judea and Galilee, cases where it is not difficult for us to imagine the direct or indirect impact on people who would have responded to Jesus' message and mission.

The Romans deliberately used *crucifixion* as an excruciatingly painful form of execution by torture (basically suffocation), to be used primarily on upstart slaves and rebellious provincials. It was usually accompanied by other forms of torture, such as severe beatings. Many of the victims were never buried but simply left on the crosses as carrion for wild beasts and birds of prey.[15] As with other forms of terrorism, crucifixions were displayed in prominent places for their "demonstration effect" on the rest of the population. (This is what the apostle Paul is referring to in his letter to the Galatians, that "Christ was publicly exhibited before your eyes as crucified" [Gal 3:1].) Seeing their relatives, friends, and other fellow villagers suffering such agonizing death would presumably intimidate the surviving populace into acquiescence in the reestablished Roman imperial order.

The Roman generals and governors assigned to Judea and Galilee repeatedly used crucifixion as a means of terrorizing the populace, presumably to deter further resistance. In retaliation for the widespread revolt in 4 B.C.E., around the time Jesus was born, the Roman general Varus, after burning towns and devastating the countryside, scoured the hills for rebels and eventually had about two thousand men crucified (*War* 2.71–76; *Ant.* 17.295). Later, Roman governors such as Felix (52–60) and Festus (60–62) crucified large numbers of brigands (bandits) as examples of how those who disturbed the imperial order in Palestine would be treated (*War* 2.253, 271). We should keep in mind, of course, that the Romans labeled everyone from vociferous protesters and actual bandits to more serious rebels as "bandits." The men also crucified along with Jesus of Nazareth, according to the Gospels, were "bandits" of some sort (not "thieves"). In a desperate attempt to humiliate and intimidate the Jerusalemites, as incidents escalated toward wider uprising in the summer of 66, the last governor, Florus, even had the temerity to beat and nail to the cross some upper-class Judeans (*War* 2.306–8).

During the Roman siege of Jerusalem toward the end of the great revolt, the Roman general Titus ordered cavalry to seize the poor people who were fleeing the besieged city.

They were accordingly beaten and subjected to torture of every description . . . and then crucified opposite the walls. Some five hundred or more were captured daily. . . . [Titus] hoped that the spectacle might induce the Judeans to surrender for fear that continued resistance would involve them in a similar fate. The soldiers out of rage and hatred amused themselves by nailing their prisoners in different postures; and so great was their number that space could not be found for the crosses nor crosses for the bodies." (*War* 5.449–51)

Even more ominous in brutality and far more extensive in reach was the Roman *systematic slaughter and mass enslavement* of subject peoples. "The aim was to punish, to avenge, and to terrify."[16] Germanicus ruthlessly slaughtered the general populace across the Rhine: "for fifty miles around he wasted the country with sword and flame. Neither age nor sex inspired pity. Places sacred and profane were razed indifferently to the ground. . . . Only the destruction of the race would end the war" (Tacitus, *Ann.* 1.51.56; 2.21). When the Nasamones revolted, Domitian simply eradicated them (Cassius Dio 67.4.6). The principal purpose, of course, was to terrorize and control subject peoples, not to annihilate all of them. Augustus articulated the principle on the monuments listing his glorious achievements: "Foreign peoples who could safely be pardoned I preferred to spare rather than extirpate."

In Palestine the brutality started soon after the initial Roman conquest in 63 B.C.E. and continued, literally, for two centuries. Two dramatic acts of gratuitous vengeance by Roman warlords must have left a collective trauma in Galilee that directly affected the Jesus movement. Eager to reassert Roman power in Palestine after the "civil war" between rival factions of the puppet Hasmonean dynasty had erupted, Cassius enslaved 30,000 people in and around Tarichaeae (i.e., Magdala) on the Sea of Galilee, in 53–52 (*War* 1.180), about fifty years prior to the time of Mary Magdalene, who, judging from her name, must have been raised there. Then, in 4 B.C.E., in vengeful retaliation against rebellion, Varus's troops burned the town of Sepphoris (and the surrounding villages?) and enslaved the inhabitants. This destruction and mass enslavement would have affected people in every village in the immediate area of Sepphoris, such as Nazareth, only a few miles away. Similarly in the

Judean hill country, Varus totally destroyed the village of Emmaus (familiar from one of the stories of Jesus' resurrection). The Roman killing or enslavement of tens of thousands of Galileans and Judeans around the time Jesus was born must have left mass trauma among the people in its wake.

The scope of the slaughter and enslavement in 4 B.C.E. pales, however, in comparison with the massacre and destruction of village after village and the mass enslavement by Roman troops in their "search-and-destroy" and "scorched-earth" practices in retaliation against the great revolt of 66–70 (described at great length by Josephus).[17] The numerous examples of massive Roman massacres and annihilations of whole peoples in retaliation for revolts and even minor breaches of treaty provide numerous parallels that make Josephus's horrifying accounts of the brutal Roman treatment of Galileans and Judeans entirely credible.

Humiliation

Like the modern Mafia, Romans apparently viewed their relationship with other peoples in terms of a competition for honor.[18] Rome asserted its superiority by humiliating its enemies, especially those who were far off, exotic, and strange. Besides being a prime form of terrorization, crucifixion was a way of utterly humiliating subject peoples. Leaving the bodies on the cross as prey for birds and beasts and without burial was the ultimate form of dehumanization. Other punitive imperial practices of the Romans, such as levying tribute and displaying the Roman army standards in the faces of their subjects, must also be seen as forms of humiliation.

We cannot possibly explain the ferocity with which the Romans retaliated against even economically insignificant cases of failure to "render unto Caesar" if the tribute was only a source of imperial revenue. For the Romans, levying tribute was evidently also a form of humiliating subject peoples. In submission the people had to render up a portion of their produce to their superior conquerors—"a sort of reward of victory and punishment for war" (Cicero, *Verr.* 2.3.12). It is impossible to separate the economic benefits of imperial domination from the symbolic value of domination and subjugation. The accumulation of the world's resources in the imperial Roman metropolis was a source of national pride. But not surprisingly, resentment was strong among subject peoples, and that in turn destabilized the imperial order, leading to revolts and devastating Roman imperial retaliation, often in an escalating spiral of violence, as in Palestine.

Forcing subject peoples to acknowledge or even worship the Roman army standards was yet another form of humiliation. The Romans used this form of humiliation particularly in treatment of Middle Eastern peoples such as the Parthians. The "arrogant" Parthian Artabanus, besides sacrificing to images of Augustus and Gaius, was forced to worship Roman military standards (Suetonius, *Gaius* 14.3). Plautius Silvanus boasted that he required foreign kings to salute the Roman military standards, apparently in deference to Roman military superiority (Tacitus, *Ann.* 15–29). Accordingly, historians may have underinterpreted an action of Pontius Pilate that must have been even more highly provocative than previously recognized. In one of his first actions when he became governor of Judea, Pilate took the bold step, in departure from the practice of previous governors, of "introducing into Jerusalem by night and under cover the effigies of Caesar which are called standards" (*War* 2.169). Surely the Judeans knew that this move by Pilate was a deliberate act of humiliation, as well as a violation of the covenantal prohibition of images. That would better explain the adamant protest that Judeans mounted against Pilate's provocation (*Ant.* 18.57–59; see further chapter 2).

INDIRECT RULE THROUGH KINGS AND HIGH PRIESTS

Once Pompey and other Roman warlords conquered various Middle Eastern peoples, they generally controlled them through indirect rule, that is, through native kings or other military strongmen. It was an "old and long-standing principle of Roman policy [to] employ kings among the instruments of servitude" (Tacitus, *Agr.* 14.1). Although the Romans often had to deploy military forces to set their client rulers in place, they could thereafter rely on the indigenous rulers to maintain order in their own realms.

When the Hasmonean high-priestly family persisted in prolonged civil war along the sensitive frontier with the Parthians, Julius Caesar and Marc Anthony chose the ruthless young military strongman Herod to control Palestine. Having become "king of the Judeans" not by the grace of God but by the designation of the Roman Senate (Josephus, *War* 1.282–85), it took Herod three years and the help of considerable Roman military aid to subdue his subjects, who put up persistent resistance. Once in control, however, he established massive military fortresses and ruled with an iron fist, allowing no dissent and requiring demonstrations of allegiance to his own and Roman rule. Indeed, Herod became the emperor Augustus's favorite client king. And well he should have been, considering his tightly repressive control of his kingdom and his massive building projects of temples and whole cities dedicated to and named for Augustus Caesar. Herod's "development" of his realm during the thirty-seven years of his rule was dramatic by ancient standards.[19]

Herod retained the high priesthood and Temple apparatus as part of his regime. After eliminating the last members of the Hasmonean family, he installed high-priestly families of his own choosing, even families from the diaspora in Egypt and Babylon. Even more ominously, he completely rebuilt the Temple in grand Hellenistic fashion. "Herod's" Temple became one of the "wonders of the world," famous as a tourist site for wealthy Romans and a pilgrimage destination for well-off Jews from diaspora communities in the Hellenistic cities of the eastern empire. That meant, however, that the Judean, Samaritan, and Galilean peasants who had previously lived under only one set of rulers, the Hasmonean high priests, were suddenly subject to three layers of rulers and the economic demands of all three: tribute to the Romans and taxes to Herod on top of the tithes and offerings to the temple-state. Herod (and his successors) also took steps to integrate Palestine into the larger imperial economy.

Herod sponsored other massive building projects throughout his realm. These included the (re)building of many military fortresses at strategic locations in his territory and Roman-style amphitheaters and temples to the emperor, as well as whole new cities in honor of and named after Augustus, such as Caesarea as a new port city on the coast and Sebaste (Greek for "Augustus") as a military colony on the former site of the sacred city of Samaria. He also on a regular basis gave elaborate gifts to the emperor and other members of the imperial family and liberal donations to a number of Greek cities (for public projects or buildings in his name). He also established a lavish court in grand Hellenistic-Roman style.[21]

As Josephus emphasizes, however, his extraordinary expenditures for all the building programs, his own lavish court, and his generous munificence to both imperial family members and to numerous Hellenistic cities simply exhausted his people economically during his long reign. His subjects, moreover, must have wondered at the strange new Hellenistic-Roman style of Herod's Temple, as well as the Roman institutions he installed at many sites in Palestine, especially the temples and cities dedicated to the divine Augustus. Toward the end of his reign Herod became more paranoid and ruthless than usual. He even ordered the execution of his elder sons, his presumed successors, of whom he had become suspicious. Augustus once quipped cleverly of his favorite client king (in Greek) that he would rather be Herod's pig (*hus*) than his son (*huios*).

After Herod's death, the Romans left the high-priestly rulers in place under the watchful eye and political-military backing of Roman governors in Judea (and Samaria). The governors usually held the power to appoint their own nominee to the high-priestly office itself, hence the high-priestly incumbents were directly beholden to the governors. The long tenure of both Caiaphas as high priest and Pilate as governor suggests that they developed a close working relationship. Archaeological explorations indicate that during Herodian and early Roman times, the wealthy high-priestly families and (probably the Herodian families as well) built ever more elaborate mansions for themselves on the hill overlooking the Temple from the west. This suggests that they became increasingly wealthy during the decades of their close collaboration with the Roman governors in the rule of Judea, Idumea, and Samaria.

In Galilee the Romans installed Herod's son Antipas. For the first time in their history the Galileans suddenly had a ruler and his administration located in Galilee itself. Indeed, in the span of only twenty years, roughly contemporary with the early life of Jesus of Nazareth, Antipas built two new cities. Having been raised and educated at the imperial court in Rome, Antipas established a Roman-style court and capital cities in rural Galilee that had previously had no city at all. From one or the other of his capital cities Antipas's administrators were in close proximity to every village in Galilee. Such immediate access to the peasant producers enabled Antipas to raise the resources for his massive building projects. This must have further exhausted the Galilean people economically, as suggested by the many references in the Synoptic Gospel tradition to debts and hunger. It is also quite conceivable that the high priests and their scribal retainers in Jerusalem were still attempting to keep a flow of tithes and offerings coming to the Temple and priesthood from Galilee, even though they no longer held jurisdiction over the area after Herod's death and during the lifetime of Jesus.

The client kings and high priests who ruled Judea and Galilee at the time of Jesus were thus integral parts of the newly established Roman imperial order in the Middle East. Other than their periodic slaughter, enslavement, and crucifixion in retaliation for rebellions, and the Roman governor's troops posted on the porticoes of the Temple at Passover time, the face that Rome presented to the Galilean and Judean people was that of the Herodian kings and the Jerusalem high priests.

In sum, the new world order established first by Pompey's victories in the east and then consolidated by Augustus brought a prolonged period of peace and prosperity for the already "civilized" Roman and Greek areas of the empire. The Pax Romana enabled the Romans to extract goods from the peoples they had subjected, in the form of tribute, in order both to support their military forces and to pacify the Roman masses with "bread and circus."

This new world order established by Rome as the only remaining superpower, however, meant disruption and disorder for subjected peoples of the Middle East such as the Judeans and Galileans. In conquering and reconquering them the Roman military forces repeatedly slaughtered and enslaved the inhabitants and destroyed their houses and villages, particularly in the areas of Jesus' activity around villages such as Nazareth and Capernaum. The Romans installed their own client rulers, the Herodian kings and the Jerusalem high priests, who both controlled the area and established an increasingly lavish lifestyle in rebuilt or newly founded cities such as Jerusalem, Sepphoris, and Tiberias. Besides the trauma of military terrorization the imperial order imposed on the Judean and Galilean people by the Romans meant multiple layers of rulers and their demands for tribute and taxes on top of the traditional expectation of tithes and offerings for the priests and Temple. The impact of western imperial control and the client rulers' attempts to integrate Palestine into the larger Roman imperial economy seriously threatened the viability and continuation of the traditional Galilean and Judean (Israelite) way of life.

RESISTANCE AND REBELLION IN JUDEA AND GALILEE

> *There is nothing to check blows like submission, and the resignation of the wronged victim puts the wrongdoer to confusion. . . . Will you alone disdain to serve those to whom the universe is subject?*
>
> —Herod Agrippa II to the people of Jerusalem, 66 C.E. (in Josephus)

The Galilean and Judean people were prominent among peoples subjugated by Rome for their persistent resistance and rebellion. There were also extensive revolts against Roman rule among the peoples subjected by Rome in Spain, Gaul, and North Africa.[1] Yet the Judeans and Galileans were perhaps the most adamant in reasserting their independence and defending their traditional way of life, persisting in their resistance for nearly two centuries before the Roman armies finally "pacified" Palestine more permanently.

THE PERSISTENCE AND SOCIAL ROOTS OF REVOLT IN ROMAN PALESTINE

Repeated Revolts

For generations both before and after the ministry of Jesus, the Galilean and Judean people mounted repeated protests and revolts against the Romans and their client rulers, the Herodian kings and Jerusalem high priests. Four widespread revolts over a period of nearly two centuries framed the many protests and resistance movements.[2]

1. When Herod, appointed "king of the Judeans" by the Roman Senate, came to conquer his realm with the help of Roman troops in 40 B.C.E., Judeans and particularly Galileans mounted repeated guerrilla battles against him. Resistance to Herod persisted for three years, with successful raids on his detachments of troops, attacks on the pro-Herod local officers and magnates, and skillful elusion of Herod's "search-and-destroy" tactics (*War* 1.314–30; *Ant.* 14.430–54).

2. At the end of Herod's tightly repressive rule in 4 B.C.E., the Jerusalem populace, reinforced by Passover pilgrims from surrounding villages, mounted a sustained protest, and revolts erupted in the countryside. In Galilee, Judas, son of the brigand chieftain Hezekiah, led peasants from the surrounding villages in an attack on the Herodian fortress at Sepphoris. Arming themselves from the royal arsenal, they also "made off with all the goods that had been seized there," that is, apparently they "took back" goods that had been seized from villagers by Herodian officers staffing the fortress at Sepphoris (in taxes? in foreclosure on loans?), goods that the rebels viewed as belonging rightfully to the people (*War* 2.56; *Ant.* 17.271–72). In the Judean hill country the shepherd Athronges and his brothers led villagers in a successful guerrilla war for three years, effectively asserting their independence of Roman rule (*War* 2.60–65; *Ant.* 17.278–84). They "vigorously attacked the Romans as well as the royal troops, both of whom they hated, the latter because of the arrogance that they had shown during the reign of Herod, and the Romans because of the injuries that they were inflicting. . . . On one occasion near Emmaus they even attacked a convoy of Roman troops bringing grain and weapons to the legion."

3. After decades of deteriorating economic conditions in Palestine and escalating political tensions between Judeans and Romans, widespread revolt erupted in Jerusalem and throughout the countryside in the summer of 66 C.E. The people of Jerusalem attacked leading high priests and their mansions. Jerusalemites and others routed Roman troops retreating from the city and killed the remaining Roman garrison left to hold the principal fortress in the city. With the Romans forcibly pushed out, the country was in effect temporarily free of imperial control. At several locations in Galilee, the people steadfastly resisted the Roman reconquest during the summer of 67. Then a sequence of peasant movements from different sections of the countryside converged on Jerusalem, as what seemed to be the obvious fortress city from which to hold out against the Romans. Once ensconced in the city, they attacked

Herodian and priestly aristocrats who had not already fled the city. Finally forced into cooperating with one another to defend against the Roman siege, the four principal peasant groups from the countryside fought valiantly until the Romans breached the walls, slaughtered the city's defenders, and destroyed the Temple.

4. Despite the crushing Roman defeat and slaughter of the people and destruction of their villages and the Temple, the Judean countryside again erupted in a prolonged revolt led by Simon bar Kokhba sixty years later (132–35 C.E.).

Israelite Tradition(s) and the Social Location of Resistance

A principal reason that Galileans and Judeans proved so persistent in rebellion against Roman imperial rule was the prominence of resistance to oppressive alien rule in Israelite tradition. The people's very origins lay in God's liberation of Israel from bondage to the pharaoh in Egypt, told repeatedly in the exodus story and celebrated annually in Passover. The founding prophet Moses and his successor Joshua mediated the covenant as a sort of social contract that would enable the people to maintain just social-economic relations in exclusive loyalty to their God. Then divinely inspired prophets such as Gideon and Deborah, announcing that God was delivering them from foreign domination, inspired the people to fight for their way of life as a free people in the hill country of Palestine. Popular leaders such as the young David, "anointed" ("messiahed") as their king by the people of Judah and Israel, led them in successful resistance to Philistine warlords. When Israel's own kings became overly exploitative, prophets such as Elijah spearheaded popular protest. Even after popular resistance no longer seemed possible, once the kings had consolidated their power, solitary oracular prophets such as Amos, Micah, and Jeremiah declared God's indictments and sentences against those kings and their officers for oppression of the people in violation of the Mosaic covenant. Moreover, just a century before the Roman takeover of Palestine, the successful Maccabean revolt against the Greek emperor Antiochus Epiphanes brought the Israelite tradition of resistance to oppressive foreign rulers to the forefront of the people's memory.

To understand how various Judean and Galilean groups responded differently to Roman imperial rule and how they drew on the Israelite tradition of resistance, we must appreciate their different positions in the overall structure of the new Roman world (dis)order in Palestine.[3]

The Herodian kings and Jerusalem high-priestly families simply collaborated in Roman rule, on which they were directly dependent and for which they were directly responsible.[4] Because of their position as client rulers for the Romans and their generally oppressive ruling practices, the Herodian kings and Jerusalem high-priestly rulers were as much the targets of popular resistance as were the Romans.

Judean scribal groups were, in effect, caught in the middle. Scribes had traditionally played an important mediating as well as governing role in Judean society under imperial rule. While wary of the power of their high-priestly patrons, on whom they were dependent economically, they provided the intellectual and administrative staff of the Temple apparatus that governed the society.[5] In that capacity they had become the principal cultivators and interpreters of the officially recognized cultural tradition of the Judean temple-state.[6] In that connection they developed a sense of their own authority, semi-independent of their high-priestly rulers-patrons, as the proper guardians of the Judean law and other cultural traditions, what anthropologists would call the "great tradition." By Roman times an officially sanctioned version of the Israelite "great tradition" had attained the sacred authority of "scripture," in the form of scrolls kept mainly in the Temple (the predecessors of what became the Hebrew Bible centuries later).[7]

Scribal administrators and advisers of the high-priestly regime could therefore easily find themselves torn between loyalty to their God as guardians of Israelite tradition and their role as mediators of the imperial order in the temple-state—particularly when the practices of Roman imperial rule and actions of the Herodian and high-priestly rulers conflicted with Israelite law and tradition. Certainly the majority of "scribes and Pharisees" adjusted their interpretation of the officially recognized "Law" to the prevailing power relations of Roman imperial rule in Judea (as portrayed in the Gospels). At points, however, some scribal teachers and circles found they could not compromise their Israelite tradition beyond a certain point, as we shall see below.

Among the ordinary people, the circumstances of the populace of Jerusalem were different from that of Judean and Galilean villagers. Many, if not most, Jerusalemites would have been economically dependent on the Temple apparatus, directly or indirectly. Through much of Herod's reign and for nearly three generations after, for example, thousands of people were employed in the massive reconstruction of the Temple complex. Like the people of any preindustrial capital city, ancient Jerusalemites would have had a vested interest in and loyalty to the ruling institutions, if not the incumbent rulers. In the Roman imperial order, however, these rulers may have been compromised in the eyes of many Jerusalemites, who might well have opted to defend their traditions against the very high-priestly officers of the temple-state.

Judean and Galilean peasants, on the other hand, lived in semi-independent village communities. As the productive economic base of the Jerusalem Temple and priesthood and of the Herodian capital cities of Sepphoris and Tiberias in Galilee, the peasants' role was to render up produce in tithes, taxes, and tribute for the rulers' support. So long as tithes and taxes were forthcoming, the Jerusalem priestly rulers and the Herodian rulers in Galilee interfered very little in the local self-governance of these village communities. Peasant villagers therefore enjoyed a degree of independent community life as well as an interest in minimizing the amount of their produce taken in taxes. Further, Judean and Galilean peasants were cultivating their own popular version of Israelite tradition that, far more than the version accepted in Jerusalem, emphasized stories of liberation from oppressive rule, popular leaders such as Elijah, and covenantal ideals of justice (which we shall explore further in chapter 3).

PROTEST, RESISTANCE, AND TERRORISM BY SCRIBAL GROUPS

Scribal resistance to the priestly rulers of the Jerusalem temple-state and their imperial sponsors emerged in a dramatic crisis about a century before the Roman takeover. When the dominant faction among the priestly rulers in Jerusalem, with the backing of the Seleucid imperial regime, in effect abandoned the traditional Mosaic Law, a circle of scribal teachers (*maskilim*) opted to resist the forced assimilation to "western" ways. Their steadfast resistance and willingness to face death as martyrs for their cause were inspired by the visions of God's deliverance of the people and vindication of the martyrs that form Daniel 7–12.

At several points during the first century of Roman imperial rule in Judea, scribal groups mounted ad hoc protests and organized resistance. Prior to the mid-first century C.E. these were all nonviolent actions, apparently in full awareness that even minimal defiance would almost certainly lead to their torture and brutal execution. In the three cases we know of from the historian Josephus, the resistance was deeply rooted in the Mosaic covenant, the very foundation of Judean society. In every case it is clear that, following the principle of exclusive loyalty to God and God's law, the religious and political-economic dimensions are inseparable.

The Qumran Community, the Pharisees, and Other Circles of Scribes/Sages

The "utopian community" near the northwest corner of the Dead Sea that left the caches of scrolls that were discovered in 1947 apparently originated in reaction to the new Hasmonean high priests' accommodation with the Seleucid Empire. This group of scribes and priests launched a new exodus into the wilderness at Qumran, where they formed a renewed covenant community. Once settled into their rigorous covenantal discipline, they intensively studied and interpreted scrolls of the Law and Prophets. They also generated an elaborate scenario of holy war against the Romans. In the scroll of "the War of the Sons of Light against the Sons of Darkness," "the Kittim" (the Romans) are seen as totally in the power of the Prince of Darkness. Although they were utterly without weapons for self-defense, the Qumranites apparently rehearsed regularly for their eventual role in the final battle where they, with the sons of light, would fight victoriously against "the Kittim" and the sons of darkness.[8]

Scribal circles that continued in their mediating role in the imperial order also mounted occasional protests. When Herod required the whole people to swear an oath of loyalty to Caesar and his own rule, the Pharisees, "over six thousand in number, refused to take the oath" (Josephus, *Ant.* 17.42). Most dramatic was a daring symbolic action taken against Herodian-Roman rule as Herod lay dying. In a vivid symbol of the subjection of the Judean people to Rome he had erected a giant golden (Roman) eagle as a votive offering over the great gate of the Temple (*War* 1.648–55; *Ant.* 17.149–67)—a constant visible reminder to the people of their subjection. Judas ben Saripha and Matthias ben Margala, "the most learned of the Judeans and unrivaled interpreters of the ancestral laws," inspired some of their students to cut down the golden eagle from atop the Temple gate, "to avenge the honor of God." Clearly the Mosaic covenantal law, which required exclusive loyalty to God as Israel's only ruler and forbade the visible representation of the divine, underlay this suicidal action in defiance of Rome's client king. In his typical brutality Herod had the scholars and those who had cut down the eagle burned alive. The martyrdom of these teachers and their students, however, inspired far wider protest among the Jerusalem populace as Herod finally died and his son Archelaus attempted to take power.

"The Fourth Philosophy"
—Refusal to Pay Tribute to the Romans

The most significant scribal action against imperial rule was led by the "Fourth Philosophy," which Josephus includes among the principal scribal factions of the Judeans.[9] When the Romans installed the "direct rule" of the Roman governors over Judea and reimposed the tribute in 6 C.E., the "teacher" Judas of Gamla and Saddok the Pharisee organized resistance (*War* 2.118). They insisted that since they owed exclusive loyalty to God as their Lord and Master, they could not render up the tribute, which meant acknowledging Caesar as lord.

> They said that such a tax assessment amounted to slavery, pure and simple, and urged the people to claim their freedom. If successful, they argued, the Judeans would have paved the way for good fortune; if they were defeated in their quest, they would at least have honor and glory for their high ideals. Furthermore, God would eagerly join in promoting the success of their plans, especially if they did not shrink from the slaughter that might come upon them. . . . The Fourth Philosophy . . . agree with the views of the Pharisees in everything except their unconquerable passion for freedom, since they take God as their only leader and master. They shrug off submitting to unusual forms of death and stand firm in the face of torture of relatives and friends, all for refusing to call any man master. (*Ant.* 18.4–5, 23)[10]

Once we translate from Josephus's Hellenistic philosophical terms back into more traditional Israelite terms, the views that they share with the Pharisees (*Ant.* 18.23) sound like the views of most Judeans and Galileans at the time. They well knew that the Romans laid subject peoples under tribute as a mark of their "slavery" and humiliation (as noted in chapter 1). But they longed to regain their freedom, as established originally in the exodus from bondage in Egypt, which they celebrated annually in the Passover festival. That God was "their only leader and master" was not only fundamental to the Mosaic covenant, in which God was understood literally as the king of Israel, but was declared in many prayers and psalms.[11] Their belief, further, that God would be concurring and collaborating in their struggle for freedom was also standard in Israelite tradition.[12] Judas, Saddok, and their cohorts, motivated by their "unconquerable passion for freedom," took direct action in the faith that God also would be acting decisively through their action to reestablish the people's freedom. In their willingness to suffer in the confidence that God would vindicate them in "honor and glory," the activists of the "Fourth Philosophy" stood in the tradition of the teachers (*maskilim*) who stood steadfast under the persecutions of Antiochus Epiphanes, inspired by the visions in Daniel 7–12.

The (Counter)Terrorism of the Sicarii

During the 50s, Josephus reports, in contrast to the highly familiar bandits based in remote rural areas, a completely "different form of 'bandits'" emerged in Jerusalem. These were the *Sicarii*, named after their curved-bladed daggers.[13] Like the Fourth Philosophy, these "daggermen" consisted of, or were led by, scribal scholar-teachers. Indeed, the leadership of the group appears to have had some continuity with that of the earlier Fourth Philosophy.[14] The tactics of the Sicarii, however, were utterly different and unprecedented in ancient Judea: surreptitious assassinations and kidnappings. Today we would call this terrorism—or, since it came in response to the brutal crucifixions and other repressive attacks with which the Roman governor was terrorizing the Judean peasantry, perhaps the more appropriate term would be counterterrorism. In both their circumstances and tactics the Sicarii resemble certain twentieth-century anticolonial terrorist movements, such as the National Liberation Front in Algeria and the Zionist Irgun Zvai Leumi in Palestine. Given their striking similarities, it makes sense to deal with these ancient Judean terrorists in comparison with studies of modern terrorist groups.[15]

People tend to resort to acts of terrorism only when previously available channels of communication have been closed off and other forms of protest have proved ineffective or futile. The situation of the Judean and Galilean peasant producers had deteriorated because of a drought and famine in the late 40s, and the ruling elite had apparently taken no steps to alleviate the desperate situation. The people had mounted numerous protests and renewal movements in recent decades, but the high-priestly rulers paid no attention. The Roman governors had been unleashing their military forces on both peaceable urban protest and unarmed movements in the wilderness led by popular prophets. During the late 40s and early 50s, the Roman governors became even more brutal in their attempts to crush any expression of unrest. By violent over-reaction, Cumanus (48–52) caused a minor incident to escalate into a major conflict involving large numbers of people, and then smashed the protests with military brutality (*War* 2.228–29; *Ant.* 20.113–14). His successor Felix (52–60) then attempted systematically to crush the spreading banditry, surely fueled by the recent famine. "Of the brigands whom he crucified, and of the common people who were suspected of being in complicity with them and punished, the number was incalculable" (*War* 2.253). With the Jerusalem high-priestly aristocracy collaborating with, rather than protesting to, the Roman governor, Roman domination seemed ever more intransigent.

According to studies of recent terrorist groups, this is just the sort of conditions that result in desperate people resorting to terrorist action as the only way of getting the attention of those who control the situation. Because nonviolent protests were merely met with further violent repression by Roman troops, the Sicarii must have felt that their only recourse was some sort of counterviolence. Being a small group of intellectuals, moreover, they had no power base among the people from which they could have built a wider movement. Also, like certain twentieth-century anticolonial movements (e.g., the Mau Mau in Kenya or EOKA in Cyprus), they targeted privileged power-holders of their own society who were collaborating in imperial rule, rather than the alien rulers themselves. Insofar as Roman imperial rule in Judea worked through the high-priestly rulers in the Jerusalem Temple, moreover, the Sicarii may have thought they were also striking symbolic blows against the empire.

The Sicarii began their campaign with selective surreptitious assassination:

> But while the countryside was thus cleared [of bandits], a different type of bandits [*heteron eidos leston*] sprang up in Jerusalem, the so-called *sicarii,* who murdered men in broad daylight in the heart of the city. Especially during the festivals they would mingle with the crowd, carrying short daggers concealed under their clothing, with which they stabbed their enemies. Then when they fell, the murderers would join in the cries of indignation and, through this plausible behavior, avoided discovery. The first to be assassinated by them was Jonathan the high priest. After his death, there were numerous daily murders. (*War* 2.254–56)

> They committed these murders . . . even in some cases in the temple. (*Ant.* 20.164–65)

Also in less clandestine fashion, says Josephus, they killed wealthy and powerful figures in the countryside and plundered their estates (*War* 7.254). These assassinations had the desired terrorizing effect. "The panic created was more alarming than the calamity itself; every one, as on the battlefield, hourly expecting death. Men . . . would not even trust their friends when they approached" (*War* 2.256–57).

These terrorist tactics, far from being irrational, were carefully calculated in terms of predictable costs, benefits, and consequences. In assassinating the high priests the Sicarii were selecting targets with maximum symbolic political value, that is, the priestly elite who were collaborating in both Roman imperial rule and its brutal treatment of the people. Besides the symbolic value of the high priests as Judean rulers and representatives of Roman rule, the Sicarii chose both a highly symbolic place, the Temple, and a highly charged time, one of the pilgrimage festivals (Passover?), to carry out their clandestine assassinations.[16] Terrorists carry out such actions primarily for their "demonstration effect," just as the Romans crucified resistant peasants to intimidate the rest of the populace. The Sicarii demonstrated that the collaborators in and beneficiaries of the Roman imperial order were vulnerable. They were also signaling to the elite of the imperial order that those subjected to the imperial order were desperate enough to take extreme action. They may also have intended their killings as punishment for previous exploitation of the people and a warning about further collaboration with the empire and mistreatment of the people.

Whether by design or not, the assassinations by the Sicarii both exacerbated the divisions among the priestly aristocracy and evoked even greater repressive violence by the elite that further polarized the deteriorating situation. The high-priestly families each assembled their own private "goon squad" for self-defense and predatory actions against the people. The high priest Ananias, for example, sent gangs of hired thugs to the threshing floors, where they forcibly expropriated the tithes intended for the ordinary priests, roughing up any peasant slow to yield up his grain (*Ant.* 20.206–7, 214). By further escalating the spiral of violence touched off by the Roman governors, the Sicarii thus contributed to the deterioration of social order in Judea that made it virtually ungovernable, which led to the outbreak of widespread revolt in 66.

POPULAR PROTESTS
—AND DISTINCTIVE ISRAELITE MOVEMENTS

Popular protests and resistance movements posed a far more serious threat to the Roman imperial order in Palestine than did the protests of scribal groups. The latter were rare, and never involved more than a tiny fraction of the overall population. Popular protests and movements were far more frequent, varied, and potentially massive. They always presented at least the threat of spreading into general popular insurrection, as indeed happened every generation or two for nearly two centuries. Every one of the popular protests or movements against Roman imperial rule surveyed below was clearly rooted in the Israelite tradition of resistance to oppressive rule and was attempting to restore the traditional Israelite way of life that had been so severely disrupted and disordered by Roman imperialism.

Protests by the Jerusalem Crowd

In ancient Jerusalem, as in other preindustrial cities without modern instruments of democracy, demonstrations or "riots" by urban "mobs" constituted the principal means by which the economically dependent populace could clamor to their rulers for redress of grievances—without for a minute challenging the ruling institutions themselves.[17] The imposition of Roman imperial rule in Judea, however, dramatically changed the situation, as can be seen in the protests of the Jerusalem crowd. The Roman imposition of Herod reduced the power and undermined the authority of the high priests, who became mere puppets of a king appointed by Rome, and after Herod puppets mere appointees of the Roman governors. Moreover, Herod eliminated all channels of political expression including public assemblies.

At end of Herod's long and oppressive reign, the pent-up resentments of the Jerusalem crowd virtually exploded. When his son Archelaus risked appearing before an assembly in the Temple courtyard in a move to consolidate support in Jerusalem for his bid to succeed his father as the Roman client king, the people pressed their grievances. They demanded that he release Herod's numerous political prisoners and that he soften his father's practice of financing "development" projects and integration into the imperial economy on the backs of the people (*Ant.* 17.204–5; cf. *War* 2.4). As symbols they seized upon the recently martyred scholars and their students who had cut down the Roman eagle from the gate of the Temple, "men who had perished on the pyre in defense of their ancestral laws and the temple" (*War* 2.5–6). The "mob" finally demanded that Archelaus purge and punish the men that Herod had appointed to positions of power and, most important of all, that he publicly remove the high priest appointed by Herod and replace him with one who "could serve more in accordance with the Law and purity" (*Ant.* 17.207). In these last demands we finally come closer to the roots of the crowd's anger: Herod's kingship and the tyrannical rule he had exercised, that is, the very key to the exercise of Roman imperial power in Judea.

Not surprisingly, at the point that the crowd more explicitly and directly challenged the very structure of the Roman imperial order in Judea—and before pilgrims from the countryside entered the city to celebrate the Passover in commemoration of their liberation from bondage in Egypt—Archelaus panicked and sent in military force. The heretofore nonviolent demonstrators rushed upon and stoned the soldiers. Archelaus then unleashed his whole army against both the demonstrators and the pilgrims entering the city for Passover, killing thousands. Yet another imperial client "king of the Judeans" had gotten his start by killing and conquering his subjects, at least those in the capital city.

A second urban protest reported by Josephus vividly illustrates the potentially explosive situation of Roman imperial rule in Judea. The annual Passover festival in which the people celebrated God's deliverance from oppressive foreign rule became a flash point for potential protest against Roman domination. In a typical imperial show of force intended for its repressive effect, the Roman governors made a practice of bringing a company of soldiers into Jerusalem and posting them "on the porticoes of the Temple so as to quell any uprising that might occur" (*Ant.* 20.106). At one Passover in the mid-first century a lewd gesture by a soldier to the crowd below touched off a vigorous and persistent protest demonstration. The governor Cumanus responded by calling out his whole army, which panicked the crowd into a stampede in which many of their number were crushed to death (*Ant.* 20.108–11). As much or more than any other protest or movement, this "riot" at the Passover festival illustrates the almost irreconcilable conflict between the relentless Roman imperial domination and the subjected Judean and Galilean people rooted in Israelite tradition adamant about independence of foreign rule.

Popular Protests in the Countryside

The most remarkable of all the popular protests by the Judean and Galilean people occurred just before and just after the mission of Jesus of Nazareth. In both cases the Roman provocation was blatant in its symbolism and extreme in its aggressive threat of lethal military violence. In both cases the Judean and Galilean people mounted massive, disciplined, nonviolent demonstrations against the provocative Roman action. And in both cases the subject people of Palestine demonstrated their own willingness to suffer and die to defend their traditional way of life, in particular, the Mosaic covenantal principle of exclusive loyalty to their God.

Prior to Pontius Pilate the Roman governors would appear to have taken into consideration the special sensitivities of the Judeans about their political-economic-religious "slavery." Shortly after he took up his duties, however, in what appears to have been a deliberate provocation, Pilate sent a company of troops into Jerusalem carrying their standards with the images of their gods on them.[18] As noted in chapter 1, the Romans often forced subject peoples to acknowledge or worship the army standards as a means of humiliation. Of all subject peoples, the Judeans would surely have been aware of the significance of the army standards. Outraged at this aggressive action that demonstrated the subjugation of their God to the Roman gods[19] and blatantly violated the Mosaic covenant commandments, large numbers of "people from the countryside," along with some Jerusalemites,

> hastened after Pilate to Caesarea [seat of the Roman governor] . . . and fell
> prostrate around his residence for five whole days. On the ensuing day Pi-
> late took his seat on his tribunal in the great stadium and summoned the
> multitude. . . . He gave the arranged signal to his armed soldiers to sur-
> round the Judeans, [who] found themselves in a ring of troops three deep.
> After threatening to cut them down if they refused to admit Caesar's im-
> ages, Pilate signaled to the soldiers to draw their swords. Thereupon the
> Judeans, as by concerted action, flung themselves in a body on the ground,
> extended their necks, and exclaimed that they were ready to die rather
> than to transgress the Law. (*War* 2.169–74; cf. *Ant.* 18.55–59)

Pilate finally relented. In a remarkably measured and disciplined mass demonstration, the Judean protesters thus demonstrated the depth of their commitment to the covenantal principles of their traditional way of life.

In a far more massive and prolonged protest about a decade later, Galilean peasants generated a widespread peasant "strike" against another Roman provocation.[20] Miffed that Jews in Alexandria had not given him the same divine honors as other subject peoples, the new emperor Gaius (Caligula) ordered his legate in Syria to set up his image in the Jerusalem Temple. If the Judeans resisted, "he was to subdue them by force of arms." Petronius advanced as far as the city of Ptolemais on the coast west of Galilee with two legions of the Roman army to prepare the military mission into Judea. Large numbers came to protest the imminent action, and large numbers of peasants refused to plant their fields and sustained the strike for weeks. As the nervous high-ranking advisers to Agrippa I (the newly appointed Herodian ruler of Galilee) pointed out, unless the peasant strike ended, there would be no crops later that year, hence no payment of tribute to Rome (and of course none for Agrippa's administration as well). Ominously, the result of Gaius's order and the popular strike would inevitably be "a harvest of banditry" (*Ant.* 18.261–74). Petronius was persuaded to defy his emperor. But Gaius's death saved him from suicide and, far more significant historically, saved Galilee and Judea from what would surely have become a revolt.

These sizable popular protests and the provocative Roman actions that touched them off are telling indicators of the intractable conflict between Roman imperial rule and the subject peoples of Palestine right around the time of Jesus' mission in Galilee. Although the Judean and Galilean peasantry were powerless against overwhelming Roman military might, they nevertheless mounted sustained demonstrations to insist on their covenantal way of life, protests that were remarkable for their size and their disciplined nonviolence and unshakable commitment.

Popular Prophetic and Messianic Movements

Many of the movements and revolts against Roman imperial rule took social forms that were distinctive to Israelite tradition and society— social forms very suggestive for their similarities to prominent themes in Jesus' preaching and practice.

The revolts that erupted in Galilee, Perea, and Judea at the death of Herod all took a readily discernible social form that could be called "messianic movements" (*War* 2.56–65; *Ant* 17.271–85).[21] Josephus writes in each case that the rebels acclaimed one of their number as "king." His deliberate choice of Hellenistic terms such as "donned the diadem" and "aspired to the kingship," however, cannot hide the Israelite tradition that underlies and informs these movements. The biblical accounts of the rise of ancient Israelite kingship in response to the threat of Philistine domination mention that first "the men of Judah . . . anointed David king" over Judah and then "all the elders of Israel anointed David king" over Israel (2 Sam 2:4; 5:3; cf. 1 Sam 11:15 on Saul; 2 Sam 15:10-12 and 19:10 on Absalom; and 1 Kgs 12:20 on Jeroboam). This is the Israelite popular tradition of the people themselves "messiahing" (=acclaiming, electing) their king on a conditional basis, not the later "great tradition" of imperial kingship of Solomon and the royal psalms (2 Samuel 7; Psalms 2; 110; 132; etc.). This popular tradition of kingship was also revolutionary, insofar as the people were "anointing" a king to lead them in their struggle for independence from oppressive domestic and foreign rulers such as the Philistines.

These movements all arose in the countryside among the peasantry. Many of them were very likely "desperate men" (*Ant.* 17.271; like the followers of David, 1 Sam 22:2), because of the deteriorating economic conditions for the peasantry under Herod. That they acclaimed a king "in their madness" and fought "with more recklessness than science" (*Ant.* 17.274–76) may indicate that they were divinely inspired. Their elected "kings" or "messiahs" were all men of humble origin. Athronges in Judea was a mere shepherd (like David in Israelite legend), Judas in Galilee was the son of the brigand chieftain Hezekiah, and Simon in Perea was a former royal servant or slave (perhaps a tenant or low-level steward on one of the royal estates).

These messianic movements had two interrelated goals: to attain freedom from Roman and Herodian rule and to restore a more egalitarian social-economic order. The virulence of their guerrilla attacks on both Herodian fortresses and Roman troops appears to have arisen from long-suppressed resentment over decades of political domination and economic exploitation under the Roman imperial order in Palestine. These movements were consciously political. They managed to take control of considerable areas of the countryside, as well as their own lives, in effective independence of Roman rule, in one case for three years. Significantly the messianic movement in Galilee was centered in villages around Nazareth just at the time Jesus was born. Popular movements led by "kings" in the role of a new David thus attest a familiar pattern deeply rooted in Israelite tradition.

The largest messianic movement, seventy years later, achieved great importance historically as the largest fighting force to resist the Roman siege of Jerusalem in 69–70. Indeed, its leader Simon bar Giora was taken to Rome and executed with great ceremony as the enemy general ("the king of the Judeans") in the triumph that the emperor Vespasian and his son Titus staged to celebrate their great victory over the intransigent Galilean and Judean people (as cited in chapter 1). In one of several parallels with the historical prototype of the popular Israelite "messiah," David ben Jesse, Simon got his start as a popular military leader (*War* 2.521). After being pushed out of the way by the high-priestly "provisional government" at the end of the summer of 66, he began building a movement in David's old territory south of Jerusalem, with a base in Hebron (*War* 4.507–13). Among other social revolutionary aspects of this movement, Simon proclaimed "liberty for slaves and rewards for the free," in fulfillment of Israelite prophetic promises (cf. Isa 11:1-9; Jer 23:5).[22] When the Roman armies finally breached the walls and destroyed the city, Simon surrendered in a highly dramatic, symbolic manner. He arose out of the ground on the site where the Temple had stood dressed in a royal purple mantle—the attire of a king, symbolism that both Judeans and Romans would have readily recognized (*War* 7.29; cf. Herod's funeral, 1.671, and the Roman soldiers' mocking of Jesus in Mark 15:16-20).

The last major Judean revolt against Roman rule also took the form of a messianic movement. This time, as we know from rabbinic literature, the king, Simon bar Kokhba, was acclaimed as "messiah" by none other than Rabbi Akiba, with explicit reference to a biblical messianic oracle (Num 24:17; Jerusalem Talmud *Ta'anit* 4.68d).

Although not historically "successful" in the long run, these popular messianic movements are highly significant for what they indicate about how the Judean and Galilean people refused to succumb to the "new world order" that Rome imposed on Palestine. That several of these movements were able to establish their independence of Roman rule for periods of two or three years indicates that the peasantry was capable of taking collective action under its own leaders. That the form assumed by these movements imitated the earlier movements led by David and other prototypical "messiahs" indicates that the Judean and Galilean people were drawing upon and solidly committed to Israelite tradition and the way of life it represented.

Several movements of deliverance from Roman imperial rule that emerged in mid-first-century Palestine took the different but still distinctively Israelite social form of popular prophetic movements.[23] The best known were the movement of the prophet Theudas, who led his followers out to the Jordan River, and the movement of the Egyptian Jewish prophet who led his followers up to the Mount of Olives. Prophets who led movements must be distinguished from prophets of another traditional Israelite type, those who simply delivered oracles of judgment or deliverance. Most significant among the latter was the peasant prophet Jesus ben Hananiah. Reminiscent of the prophet Jeremiah's declaration of doom over Jerusalem, Jesus wandered the alleyways of Jerusalem in the years before the great revolt sounding a repeated lament over the city: "A voice from the east, a voice from the west, a voice from the four winds; a voice against Jerusalem and the temple" (Josephus, *War* 6.300–301). Although the Jerusalem priestly aristocracy wanted Jesus ben Hananiah executed, the Roman governor simply ordered him severely beaten and released, believing that he was merely deranged.

By contrast, the prophets such as Theudas and "the Egyptian" inspired and led mass movements that were quickly destroyed by the Roman military as serious threats to the imperial order. Indeed, we can discern in these movements a common pattern. According to Josephus's multiple accounts, prophets such as Theudas and "the Egyptian" led new actions of deliverance that involved "revolutionary changes" in accord with God's "design" and that corresponded to one of the great historical acts of deliverance led by Moses and Joshua. Like several other prophetic figures who led their followers out into the wilderness in anticipation of new divine acts of deliverance, Theudas "led the masses to follow him to the Jordan River," stating that "at his command the river would be parted and would provide them an easy passage" (*Ant.* 20.97). In similar fashion, "a man from Egypt," claiming that he was a prophet, led his followers up to the Mount of Olives, "asserting that at his command Jerusalem's walls would fall down," providing them an entrance into the city (*Ant.* 20.169–70; cf. *War* 2.259–62).[24] Theudas's movement is clearly patterned after either the exodus led by Moses or entry across the Jordan River into the land—or both, since they had often been conflated in Israelite tradition during the intervening centuries. The prophet "from Egypt" patterned his movement after the battle of Jericho led by Joshua. These mid-first-century prophetic movements were thus informed by and patterned after the formative acts of liberation and entry into their land in which Israel had been formed as a people.

The distinctively Israelite form taken by these prophetic movements indicates that resistance to Roman imperial rule was strongly rooted in Israelite popular tradition. That several such movements occurred in the mid-first century among the Judean peasants (and at least one among the Samaritans as well) indicates that the currents of attachment to Israelite tradition of independence and of commitment to the traditional Israelite way of life were running wide and deep in popular social memory and desire. Large numbers of peasants in different regions of the countryside were clearly yearning for new liberation from foreign bondage (as the Israelites of old had in Egypt) and/or for retaking control of their land from the rulers who were occupying it (as the Israelites of old did in the original establishment of independence in the land). Like the politically more "realistic" messianic movements, they sought to renew a more egalitarian Israelite life in defiance of the Roman new world order.

That so many movements could take one or another of the same two social forms, as "popular prophetic movements" or "popular messianic movements" with features that resemble earlier Israelite movements portrayed at certain points in the Hebrew Bible, gives evidence of a popular tradition among the Judean and Galilean peasantry.

Hidden Forms of Resistance

In all likelihood the popular protests and movements for which we have written accounts represent only the tip of the iceberg of popular resistance to Roman rule. Peasants, who were not literate, of course, left no records of their own views and actions. And only some of the popular movements that seemed to pose a serious disturbance to the established order ever "made the papers" of the accounts of ancient historians such as Josephus. Even more important perhaps is that standard historical accounts tend to focus only on overt actions of popular resistance. Recent studies of modern peasantries have discerned that active protests and movements form only the historically visible small fraction of the far wider and deeper popular resistance that remains purposely hidden.[25] In order to protect their own minimal subsistence, the always marginal peasants regularly sequestered portions of their crops before the tax collectors arrived or found various ways of sabotaging the exploitative practices of their rulers.

Furthermore, in order to appreciate the depth of popular resistance in ancient Palestine (or any comparable situation) we must recognize that all forms of protest and resistance, hidden or overt, are rooted in what has been called the "hidden transcript" of the subject people. Anthropologist and political scientist James C. Scott developed the distinction between the "public transcript" and the "hidden transcript" to illuminate different kinds of communication that take place in the conflictual dynamics of power relations between the dominant elite and the people subordinated to them.[26] Much of the behavior and speech of slaves, peasants, and workers is coerced. The open interaction and communication between the powerful and the subordinated Scott called the "official transcript," which is determined by the elite. Thus most of our written sources, which represent this "official transcript," tell only part of the historical story of power relations, from the viewpoint of the powerful. However, "every subordinate group creates, out of its ordeal, a 'hidden transcript' that represents a critique of power spoken behind the back of the dominant," in sequestered sites. Behind the few actions of the subordinate against the powerful that do "make the papers" (the written historical record produced by the elite) lies "a far more elaborate hidden transcript, an entire discourse, linked to . . . culture, religion, and the experience of colonial rule." The importance of the hidden transcript cultivated by the peasantry in their village communities behind the backs of their landlords or rulers was in keeping anger and resentment alive and focused among the subordinate. That provided the soil from which everyday forms of hidden resistance and occasional movements of protest and resistance sprang.

This survey of resistance by both Judean scribal teachers and Galilean and Judean peasants indicates conditions of persistent political unrest and agitation in Palestine under early Roman rule. The principal division was clearly between the peasantry and their rulers, Herodian and high-priestly as well as Roman, not between "Romans" and "Jews" generally. The fragmentary sources for most of the protests and resistance movements, both scribal and popular, indicate that they were rooted in and acting in defense of the traditional Israelite way of life, particularly the principles of the Mosaic covenant and memories of God's earlier acts of deliverance. Yet there is little to suggest that they were acting in defense of the Temple. Only the teachers and their students who cut down the Roman eagle over the Temple gate, and possibly the peasant strike occasioned by Caligula's provocative move to place his statue in the Temple, suggest some interest in the Temple as an important symbol. The Fourth Philosophy's resistance to the Roman tribute set them against the high priests in charge of the Temple, and nearly all the peasant movements were explicitly or implicitly acting against the Temple and high priesthood as well as against Roman rule. The peasant refugees of northwest Judea who converged on Jerusalem in 67–68 and formed the "Zealot" movement occupied the Temple Mount as the principal fortress in which they could hold out against the imminent Roman siege—in opposition to (and by) the priestly aristocracy. In some of the western areas of the Roman Empire many of the revolts involved a whole people against Roman rule. In Palestine, where the Romans simply co-opted and supplemented ruling institutions already in place from previous empires, the basic political-economic division set the people against the "native" as well as the Roman rulers. A key factor in the unusual intensity and persistence of Judean and Galilean resistance to the Roman order was the deep current of resistance to foreign domination in Israelite cultural tradition.

TOWARD A RELATIONAL
APPROACH TO JESUS

*This huge task, which consists of re-introducing mankind into the world,
the whole of mankind, will be carried out with the indispensable help of
the European peoples, who themselves must realize that in the past they
have often joined the ranks of our common masters where colonial questions are concerned. To achieve this, the European peoples must first de-
cide to wake up and shake themselves, use their brains, and stop playing
the stupid faun of the Sleeping Beauty.*

—**Frantz Fanon**

The standard approach in investigations of the historical Jesus com-
pounds the depoliticizing effects of modern Western individualism and
the separation of religion from political-economic life (discussed in the
introduction). Interest in "the historical Jesus" arose in response to the
European Enlightenment, which sharpened eighteenth- and nine-
teenth-century intellectuals' awareness of the historical difference between the past and modern culture. The Enlightenment reduction of
reality to what fit the canons of Reason and Nature, however, left theologians embarrassed about the Christian Gospels as sources for the
historical Jesus. There was altogether too much of the fantastic and
miraculous in the Gospel stories of Jesus. By the twentieth century critical theologians realized that the Gospel writers, with their own faith
perspectives and axes to grind, had provided the overall framing of the
Gospel stories. The only reliable materials that could meet modern scientific criteria for historical evidence were the sayings of Jesus, which
had to be rescued from their literary context and tested by various criteria for their "authenticity."

Recent studies of the historical Jesus, refining the approach established earlier in the twentieth century, continue to focus on the individual sayings of Jesus. Most do acknowledge that Jesus must have

performed healings and exorcisms, despite the unreliability of any particular miracle story as historical evidence. But recent interpreters of Jesus still focus primarily on the sayings of Jesus isolated from literary context, and thus also historical social-political context.

There are two fundamentally crippling problems with this procedure. First, since no one communicates in isolated sayings, this approach focuses on artificial fragments that never could have constituted units of communication, anywhere, anytime. Second, since the meaning of a saying or story always depends on a meaning context, the standard practice of taking the sayings of Jesus out of their literary context leaves the modern interpreters with no indication from the original historical context as to their meaning. Like museum curators, scholarly interpreters arrange the decontextualized artifacts by type and topic (children, meals, kingdom, wisdom), like pottery fragments displayed in museum cases by types (lamps, vases, pots, jars). The topical arrangement of Jesus sayings by scholarly interpreters in the chapters of books about Jesus has only the most general relation to the historical circumstances in which Jesus lived. The result is a Jesus who indeed spoke sayings, but was not communicating something significant to particular people in a concrete historical situation, that is, a dehistoricized "talking head."

Such crippling problems of the standard approach to the historical Jesus call for a far more elaborate and comprehensive critique than I can carry out here. But we can perhaps, in a provisional way, discern some of the contours of a more adequate, relational, and contextual approach to Jesus as a significant historical figure.

MULTIPLE ASPECTS IN CONSIDERING A HISTORICAL LEADER

Imagine reading a book entitled *The Historical Abraham Lincoln: The Life of a North American Illinois Citizen* based almost exclusively on separate statements purposely removed from literary and social context, such as the Gettysburg Address. Or imagine a book called *The Historical Martin Luther King: The Life of a North American Georgia Black Citizen* based exclusively on his statements taken out of the context of his sermons and speeches at mass rallies in the civil rights movement.[1] From their statements alone we would have no adequate sense of the historical figure of Lincoln or King or of why they were historically significant.

An adequate approach to significant historical figures such as Lincoln or King would have to consider far more than just their sayings. We would also have to consider the particular historical circumstances in which they operated, along with the other historical players and historical forces, and the major problems that the society was dealing with, in order to understand the historical crisis they faced and the possibilities of leadership. We would have to consider how such leaders interacted with the people in general in mobilizing forces or particular followers in forming a movement. The leaders' interaction with followers suggests two other crucial aspects. We also need to consider the office they held or the role(s) they played and the cultural tradition out of which leaders and followers worked in order to understand the leadership they exercised and the historical influence they had. Thus, as a significant historical figure, (1) in the mid-nineteenth-century crisis in U.S. history over the issues of slavery and the preservation of the Union, (2) working out of the previous U.S. history of freedom and slavery and constitutional tradition, (3) Abraham Lincoln, (4) as president of the United States, (5) led the Northern states to war against the Confederacy and issued the declaration of the emancipation of the slaves—and in that complex context his assassination made him a revered martyr for the cause. Similarly, as a significant historical figure, (1) at a crisis in American history over equal political rights and race relations, (2) working out of the previous history of ideals of freedom versus slavery and segregation, (3) Martin Luther King, (4) adapting the role of black preacher into that of the most prominent leader of the civil rights movement, (5) helped lead the struggle for equal political rights and more just race relations—and in that complex context his assassination made him a revered martyr for the cause.

By analogy, we can attempt to devise a more adequate, relational-contextual approach to the historical Jesus that considers five interrelated aspects. We attempt to understand how, (1) in the particular historical conditions that had created a crisis for the ancient Judean and Galilean people (2) and working out of the Israelite cultural tradition in which those people were rooted, (3) Jesus emerged as a leader (4) by assuming/adapting particular social role(s) (5) in interaction with particular people who responded by forming a movement that became historically significant—and in that complex context his crucifixion at the hands of the Romans made him a revered martyr for the cause.

This five-aspect scheme of historical investigation includes important relational and contextual factors that have often been underplayed or ignored when dealing with Jesus.[2] Any historical figure is significant historically only insofar as she or he interacted and resonated with other people in decisive ways in a particular historical situation. Almost by definition, a leader is someone who decisively influences (persuades, inspires, organizes) followers in a seriously problematic historical situation in such as way that they gain new perspective and take decisive action. A historical figure such as Jesus therefore can be approached only through the results of his interaction with people who responded to him in decisive ways in their particular historical conditions (aspect 5).

Furthermore, both leader and followers come to a historical situation out of a particular cultural tradition. Their cultural tradition determines both the repertoire of ideas and the manner of social interactions by which they will respond to the problems in their historical situation (aspect 2). In situations of cultural and political conflict, leader and followers adapt and create on the basis of their cultural tradition, often in interaction with an invasive alien culture. Moreover, leaders and followers interact in adaptation of certain roles indicated in their cultural tradition. In some cases these are institutionalized offices, as in Abraham Lincoln as president of the United States. In other cases the interaction of leader and followers takes shape more informally, by adapting certain roles or "scripts" given in the cultural tradition, such as Martin Luther King's and his followers' adaptation of the black preacher role (aspect 4).

With an approach that incorporates investigation of these five aspects it may now be possible to bring together two heretofore largely separate lines of investigation. First, recent investigations have led to a more precise sense of the historical political-economic context of Jesus' mission and movement. These enable us to cut through the false assumptions and vague constructs that have been blocking the way toward historical understanding. Second, criticisms of the methodological individualism and atomization of much recent "research" on Jesus points the way to a historically grounded sense of how to use our Gospels and gospel traditions as sources for Jesus-in-movement.

HISTORICAL CONDITIONS
AND CULTURAL TRADITIONS

Since they existed prior to Jesus, we begin with the historical conditions of (and for) Jesus' mission and the movement it generated and the cultural tradition out of which they emerged. Both the historical conditions and the conditioning culture are known from sources other than the Gospels, which form our only sources for Jesus and his movement(s).

Historical Conditions of and for Jesus-in-Movement in Roman Palestine

Class and Regional Divisions. The principal division in Palestine in Jesus' day was between the rulers, Roman, Herodian, and priestly, on the one hand, and the ordinary people, peasants, and the populace of Jerusalem and other cities, on the other (as indicated in the historical survey in chapters 1 and 2).[3] As in other areas of the Roman Empire, a huge chasm separated those of wealth, privilege, and power from those who produced for and otherwise served the desires of the ruling groups.

Regional differences between Galilee and Judea, particularly its capital, Jerusalem, rooted in their divergent histories, compounded the primary division between rulers and ruled.[4] According to "biblical" history, after the northern Israelites rebelled against the Davidic monarchy and its Temple in Jerusalem, Galilee was independent of Jerusalem rule for eight hundred years before the later Hasmonean kings–high priests took over control of the area in 104 B.C.E. Then, after only a hundred years of Jerusalem rule, first by the high priests and then by Herod, the Romans appointed Herod's son Antipas as ruler in 4 B.C.E. Galilee was thus under Jerusalem rule for the century before Jesus, but no longer under Jerusalem's jurisdiction precisely during the lifetime of Jesus.

The different histories of Judea and Galilee prior to the generation of Jesus and the political situation during his lifetime pose serious questions that New Testament scholarship has not recognized, much less explored. First, we need to refine our conceptual apparatus. Attempting to break with centuries of anti-Semitism in the wake of the Holocaust, Christians have begun to think in terms of Jesus having been a "Jew." "Outsiders to Palestine," such as the Romans, may have thought of all peoples living under Herod and later Herodian rulers as "Judeans."

"Insiders" such as the Judean historian Josephus, however, clearly distinguished the Samaritans and Galileans to the north from the Judeans proper. Later rabbinic literature assumed that the people of Galilee were Israelite in heritage, while having some customs, laws, and practices different from those of the Judeans.[5] Yet Galileans who had only recently become subjected to the Temple and high priests' demands for tithes and offerings may well have had rather ambiguous feelings about the Jerusalem rulers.[6]

Fundamental Social Forms. In one of the most serious omissions, studies of the historical Jesus have failed to investigate the fundamental social forms within Galilean society. The Galileans among whom Jesus worked, indeed the vast majority of people in any traditional agrarian society, would have been embedded in households and villages. Villages were communities of families or households engaged in subsistence agriculture (and/or fishing), a substantial percentage of whose produce was expropriated by their rulers. These rulers intervened in village affairs mainly to extract their tax revenues. Otherwise the villages were semi-autonomous communities whose religious-political form of governance was a village assembly, *knesset* in Aramaic, *synagōgē* in Greek, led by the village elders.[7]

Conditions under Roman Rule. Peasants are by definition always under the political-economic rule and exploitation of landlords or rulers.[8] As comparative studies have shown, however, protests, renewal movements, and revolts tend to arise when actions by the rulers impact village communities so severely as to cause their nascent disintegration. The Roman conquests and installation of Herodian client kings apparently had just such an impact on Galilean villagers.[9] The cumulative effect of this impact developed in three discernible stages over a period of three generations.

First, in the two generations prior to Jesus, the slaughter, enslavement, and devastation wrought by the Roman warlord Crassus in 52 in Magdala, by the Rome-appointed "king" Herod in 40–37, and by the Roman reconquest of the area near Nazareth in 4 B.C.E. would have left collective social trauma as well as physical destruction in their wake. Second, after finally conquering the country over which the Romans had named him king, Herod the Great established a rigorous administration that must have taken revenues from Galilee far more effectively than had the Hasmoneans. Third, Herod's son Antipas became the first ruler of Galilee to locate his administration directly in Galilee, making him far more capable of rigorous collection of revenues than previous rulers. Antipas needed revenue, given his costly construction of two new capital cities, Sepphoris and Tiberias. Between them, these Roman-style administrative cities built by the Rome-educated Antipas held a commanding view of nearly every village in Lower Galilee. As we are reminded by scholars of peasant societies, the rigor of tax collection can have a far more serious impact on villagers than the official rate of taxation.[10]

Thus during the generations before Jesus and especially during the first two decades of Jesus' generation, the Roman client rulers Herod and Antipas ratcheted up the economic pressure on the villages of Galilee. The distress in families and village communities, however, would have been more complex than economic deprivation by itself. For economic hardship would have quickly resulted in social disintegration as well. Under pressure, families that had extended loans to other families would themselves have come to need repayment in order to survive. But the debtors would have been unable to repay. Ordinary jealousies and backbiting in the village community would have escalated into more serious conflicts. Families that had fallen heavily into debt would have been vulnerable to their creditors, who were most likely the Herodian elite, taking control of the production process, perhaps even taking their land outright. Studies of other peasantries have shown that the most likely to respond to leaders and form movements are not the people who have lost their ancestral fields, but villagers who feel threatened by tightening circumstances that drive them into debt and hunger.

Cultural Tradition

Although nearly all Galilean villagers would have been nonliterate, they were by no means culturally ignorant. We are beginning to recognize that Galileans such as Jesus and his followers would not have known the same Torah/Law in the same way as the "scribes and Pharisees" in Jerusalem. As anthropologists have recognized for some time, village communities cultivate and live out of a "little tradition," in contrast with the elite, who cultivate the "great tradition." The "little" or popular tradition(s) in Galilee would have informed and guided "the distinctive patterns of belief and behavior valued by the peasantry" of those agrarian societies. The popular tradition, consisting of stories, laws, customs, prayers, and so on, would have been cultivated in oral communication in village communities. The corresponding "great" tradition of the Jerusalem elite existed partly on written scrolls as well as in oral cultivation mainly by scribal-scholarly circles.[11]

Through the mediation of the "scribes and Pharisees," the guardians and interpreters of the great, official tradition, there was likely some interaction between the two. But as anthropologists have found in comparative studies, the little tradition often diverges widely from the great tradition. Traditional agrarian societies such as Judea and Galilee, of course, had no integrative mechanisms comparable to those of modern societies, such as the mass media. Thus one often finds in village culture "a pattern of structural, stylistic, and normative opposition to the politico-religious tradition of the ruling elites."[12] Indeed, the symbolic and material domination exercised by rulers and their institutions seems to "engender a set of contrary values which represent in their entirety a kind of 'shadow society.'"[13]

We thus have no reason to believe, either by direct evidence or by analogy from comparable peasant societies, that Galilean peasants would have known Israelite tradition in the form cultivated by the scribes and Pharisees, much less in the form that we know it (the Hebrew Bible). Yet there are many indirect indications that the popular tradition of the Galileans as well as the Judeans was predominantly Israelite. From incidents in Galilee reported by Josephus it is evident that village interaction was guided by the Mosaic covenantal tradition, and that Galileans applied those same norms and laws to the elite, of whose behavior they were suspicious.[14] From various sources we have reason to believe that Galileans cultivated memories of Israelite heroes such as Moses and Elijah.[15] The multiple movements in Galilee, Samaria, and particularly Judea that took the forms of popular messianic movements and popular prophetic movements (sketched in chapter 2) were all informed by the Israelite "little tradition." Those movements thus provide clear evidence that Israelite stories of Moses and Joshua and of Saul and David were very much alive in the villages of Palestine.

That Judean and Galilean society as a whole continued to observe the traditional Mosaic covenantal provisions of leaving the land unplanted and canceling debts every seventh year provides a clear indication that

other provisions of the Mosaic covenantal mechanisms of ordering social-economic life were operative in village communities. That is, besides the more familiar Decalogue prohibitions of coveting, stealing,
and murder, village communities continued to cultivate and practice the
additional covenantal principles of mutual economic cooperation and
covenantal mechanisms to mitigate exploitation, such as encouragement
of mutual lending to those in need, prohibitions against interest, and
regular sabbatical cancellation of debts. This is made all the more credible by studies of other peasant societies, which have closely comparable
mechanisms to keep the constituent families of the village economically
viable, especially during hard times—what has been called the "moral
economy of the peasant."[16]

DISCERNING JESUS-IN-MOVEMENT
IN GOSPEL SOURCES

We can now attempt to bring together with this more precise sense of
historical conditions and cultural tradition in Roman Galilee and Judea
a more historically grounded sense of how to use the Gospels and gospel
traditions as sources for how Jesus, adapting a distinctive role, formed a
movement in interaction with Galileans in that context.

The Gospels as Communication
and Historical Sources

The standard approach treats the sayings of Jesus as artifacts that have
meaning in themselves. But in real life no one communicates in isolated
sayings. Communication involves other people in particular social contexts. In isolating Jesus' sayings from their literary context in the
Gospels, however, the standard procedure dispenses with our principal
guide to the historical contextual and relational meaning of Gospel materials. The speech and action of Jesus as a historical figure would have
been remembered in the first place only if they had significance for
someone. That significance lay in the communication between Jesus and
those with whom he interacted in historical context. The Gospels are
the principal results and records of such communication.

The Gospels—certainly the earliest identifiable layers in the Synoptic Gospel tradition, the Gospel of Mark and the series of Jesus'

speeches that appear in parallel passages in Matthew and Luke, known as "Q" (German *Quelle,* "source")[17]—were also oral communication. It has long been accepted that Gospel materials existed in oral form before being included in written Gospels. We are recently coming to realize, however, that in the predominantly oral communication environment of antiquity, there was no significant "great divide" between orality and literacy.[18] Long after the earliest discernible Gospel documents existed in written form, those texts still functioned as oral communication, in performance before groups or communities. That the Gospels still functioned as oral communication in community contexts gives us all the more motivation to try to transcend the modern assumptions of print culture and to reimagine how the earliest Gospels and Gospel materials "worked" as communication. Biblical interpreters, who have a strong vested interest in sacred *texts*, have been slow to come to grips with Gospel materials as communication. But some help is available from other fields, such as sociolinguistics and recent studies of oral performance.[19] Coincidentally, moreover, the theory and models of communication developed in those fields fit well with the relational-contextual approach that it is necessary to pursue adequate historical inquiry (as outlined above).

Virtually any communication, but particularly oral performance, with or without a written text, is inherently relational and embedded in social context and cultural tradition. A performance involves an audience, who participate in and contribute to a performance through their interaction with the performer. The performer recites a *text*, the performance takes place in a *context* (place, group, occasion, historical circumstances), and the recitation of the "text" resonates with/in the hearers by referencing the *tradition* in which they (and the performer) are rooted. Meaning, in oral performance, is not a "what," some meaning-in-itself to be discerned through detached reflection, but a significant relationship that happens between recited *text* and audience in a *context* and the cultural *tradition* in which they are embedded. As modern historical analysts and interpreters of ancient "texts," therefore, we must attempt to appreciate meaning as significant communication. This way of approaching the Gospels provides us a way of appreciating the meaning generated in the audience in its historical context. Since the Gospels are the results and records of what became significant communication of Jesus with his followers, they are also sources for a relational-contextual understanding of Jesus' mission. This may become clearer with a few further reflections on the various components of (oral) communication.

"Text" (the Message in Communication)

A performer or "reader" recites a particular *message*, in a particular context, which resonates with an audience out of their common cultural tradition. Even in modern print culture it is evident, on a moment's reflection, that the meaningful unit of communication is the overall message of which particular statements are components. Our communications approach to the Gospels as sources in our relational approach to Jesus must begin with consideration of what constituted the fundamental units of communication. Only on the basis of meaning in literary context can we then move to the broader historical social context, with the help of other literary sources and material (archaeological) sources.

In one promising development, some who study "Q" (the "source" behind the parallel speech-material of Jesus in Matthew and Luke that they did not get from Mark) have recognized that it is not a collection of separate sayings, but a sequence of Jesus' speeches on various subjects of concern to communities of a movement attached to Jesus.[20] But is the unit of communication then a particular speech, such as Jesus' sending out envoys on mission, or the whole sequence of speeches that comprise Q? It may be even more difficult to discern the basic unit of communication in the Gospel of Mark. Mark tells a whole story. Yet that story consists of a sequence of episodes. Is it possible that at least certain sets of episodes or even some of the individual episodes were also units of communication that functioned outside of the gospel story as whole? Did other combinations of such episodes comprise units of communication among Jesus' followers (communities/movements)?

We may get a bit closer to "texts" that were performed or read aloud to groups, such as Q and the Gospel of Mark, by analogy with performances of "oral derived texts" in other societies. For example, Old English poets or South Slavic epic singers insisted that their "words" were not only and not primarily individual statements or lines, but whole speeches, scenes, or even lengthy songs or narrative poems. By analogy, we might imagine that both particular speeches in Q (such as the mission discourse) and the overall sequence of speeches (Q as a whole), and perhaps the particular episodes as well as the overall story in Mark, were "texts" (meaningful messages).[21]

We may gain another angle on the issue from a study of Lushootseed narratives (of Salish people in the Puget Sound area). The storyteller would never tell all of the rich collection of stories and songs on one occasion. Different storytellers and even the same storyteller had different versions of a given story. By analogy we might suggest that Q and Mark represent particular "texts" composed from a far wider and richer repertoire of Jesus-speeches and Jesus-episodes known in the Jesus movement(s) and that the parallel speeches about Beelzebul, mission, and "followers on trial" found in Mark and Q were different versions of particular components of that wider repertoire of Jesus-speeches and episodes.[22]

Yet another set of observations about comparative performances may also shed light on our potential understanding of what constitutes the "text" in the cases of Q and Mark as sources for Jesus-and-followers. South Slavic singers and other performers, while insisting that they were singing the exact same "text" with no variations, in fact presented different-length recitations and variations in the wording of particular episodes while maintaining the same basic overall story line across different performances.[23] This has two important implications for Q and Mark as "texts." First, it suggests that even though particular component speeches of Q and particular episodes in Mark may have constituted basic messages or units of communication in themselves on occasion, they would usually have constituted components of a larger message/text of which Q and Mark (as we have them) are examples (the only ones known to us). That is, component speeches and episodes were usually combined in some way and had their meaning in connection with others in a sequence or narrative. Second, it is the overall story in Mark and a full series of speeches in Q that were the basic or most important messages/units of communication.

All the factors we have considered indicate that meaningful communication is carried or evoked by "texts"/messages that are much larger and more complex than individual sayings. Far from focusing on isolated individual sayings and episodes, therefore, we must focus on the overall series of speeches in Q and the overall story in Mark, in order to understand not only the whole picture but also the way each component of the overall series or story functioned in and helped constitute the whole picture.

Thus, even if we were to conclude that—in addition to Mark as a whole and Q as a whole—particular speeches in Q and particular episodes or combinations of episodes in Mark did constitute units of communication, then the overall literary context of those smaller units of communication constitutes our principal (or only) guide to the units' meaning context. For two very basic reasons, therefore, historical inquiry about Jesus-in-context must begin by focusing on whole documents. Since, by general scholarly consensus, Q and Mark were the earliest "documents," we will focus on them in this investigation.

In this connection the recent revival of literary analysis of the Gospels, despite being relatively oblivious to historical considerations, may be of help to a historical reading. In reading Mark as an overall narrative, we must deal with the plot, which includes the political conflict(s) in the story. And the plot and subplots of the story that involve political conflict, such as that between Jesus and the Jerusalem rulers as well as the Pharisees, drive us right back into the historical context. Moreover, the historical context in which Mark and Q were produced and which they addressed appears to be relatively close, historically, to that of Jesus and his immediate followers. Recent investigations into their respective original contexts conclude that Q was located in Galilee or nearby, roughly a generation after Jesus, and Mark probably in southern Syria either just before or just after the great revolt in 66–70. In both cases this brings us into or close to the same Galilean and Syrian village community context that Jesus worked in just a few decades earlier, so that many of the same aspects of the historical context sketched above pertain to Mark and Q as well as to Jesus.

Context (of Communication)

A performer recites and an audience hears a message in a particular *context*. In fact, context determines what is to be communicated and context cues the audience into hearing what is communicated in a certain way. At a funeral we expect to hear music and discourse appropriate to a funeral, and the presiding priest or minister prepares a message of consolation and eulogy. At a protest demonstration we would not expect to hear words of praise for the target of the protest. Complex texts, however, may have a variety of contexts at different times or levels. For example, the overall context of the Mass or a church worship service in which the overall liturgy is recited includes several subcontexts of praise, confession, words of assurance, hearing of the word, preaching, and the offering of the people. As the worshipers shift from one subcontext to another, the register of the messages changes accordingly. Something similar happened in civil rights rallies, with their different subcontexts of singing freedom songs, remembering fallen comrades, or hearing an inspiring exhortation to continue the struggle.

We can detect something similar with regard to the sequence of speeches in Q. The context of the overall series of speeches must have been community meetings of a Jesus movement. Within those meetings, however, must have been subcontexts, such as a commissioning of envoys as the subcontext of the mission discourse, or preparation for group prayer as the subcontext of the short speech on prayer (including the Lord's Prayer). The context for hearing the Gospel of Mark must also have been community meetings of a Jesus movement.[24]

In attempting to understand the Gospels in historical context and as sources for Jesus-in-context, however, we must consider a much wider context of communication. The Gospels, Q and Mark in particular, were the communicative products and media of a recently arisen, dynamic, and growing movement. For the movement to have begun in the first place and to have rapidly expanded, the message must have resonated with people who formed or joined the movement and must have continued to resonate with the people who participated in the movement. We must thus consider the historical social context as well as the community/movement context. For example, beyond the immediate context of a Jesus movement's meeting to commission envoys to expand Jesus' project of preaching and healing we must consider the historical context (crisis) that led them to begin and to continue sending out such envoys. Or, more broadly, besides the community meetings in which the Gospel of Mark or Q was recited, we must consider the historical crisis in response to which the Gospel and the Q speeches originated and which they continued to address, in which expanding numbers of people resonated to those texts in expanding communities. We want to understand why such messages resonated with certain people in a certain historical crisis.

Tradition

The text/message resonates with the hearers by referencing the cultural *tradition* in which they live. Even those of us whose lives are spent predominantly in print culture have experiences that illustrate what is usual in oral communication. Hearing (on the radio or TV) even a brief sound bite of Martin Luther King's voice saying, in his inimitable preaching style, "I have a dream," evokes memories of the whole civil rights era for Americans who lived through the 1960s. For those who were deeply involved in the struggle for civil rights, hearing King's voice may even evoke profound feelings, vivid memories of particularly tense confrontations, and a recommitment to the values represented by the freedom movement. Even an orally voiced written text of Abraham Lincoln saying "Four score and seven years ago" evokes in memory not only the larger text of the Gettysburg Address, but a whole important segment of American cultural tradition. What all of these examples illustrate is how even a fragment from a performed "text" resonates in the hearers by referencing their cultural memory and tradition.

The key to how the text resonates with the hearers by referencing the cultural tradition is that a part stands for the whole, metonymically. "I have a dream" evokes the whole African American struggle for civil rights. When the Gospel of Mark tells of Jesus making sea crossings and performing feedings in the wilderness when no food was available it evokes in those hearers the whole Israelite tradition of Moses leading the exodus and the arduous journey of Israel through the wilderness toward their land. Even before the audience hears that Moses and Elijah appeared with the transfigured Jesus on the mountain, the text of Mark has given the audience unmistakable clues that Jesus is a prophet like Moses and Elijah leading a renewal of Israel. This illustrates how the audience interprets the text on the basis of the shared body of knowledge that is their cultural tradition. Or, to state that more comprehensively than its surface cognitive dimension, the portrayal of Jesus making sea crossings and wilderness feedings, by referencing the hearers' shared Israelite cultural tradition, evokes in the audience the confidence or trust/faith that Jesus was another prophet like Moses who was carrying out a new deliverance of Israel from foreign oppression.[25]

Again we are being driven to an approach virtually the opposite of that previously pursued by standard Gospel studies and research into the historical Jesus. Although scholars of the historical Jesus were students of the Enlightenment in their rationalistic assessment of the Gospels as historical sources, they retained basic theological assumptions and agenda. In traditional Christian theology, Jesus was the agent and mouthpiece of revelation. Under the influence of Enlightenment reason, revelation was understood especially in terms of teachings. Revelation, of course, meant something new, something that had not been heard or known before. Insofar as modern scholars focused on the isolated sayings of Jesus, that meant the sayings in themselves had to be new, and somehow revelatory. (That is a tall order!) Almost by definition Jesus' teachings had to be new over against "Judaism" (and the subsequent "early church"). Thus, using the criterion of "dissimilarity," Jesus scholars researched Jewish literature not to understand Jesus' teachings in their historical context, but rather to set the "authentic" sayings over against "conventional" Jewish norms, customs, and other cultural content.

In a relational-contextual and communications approach, revelation would have to be understood relationally-historically. Revelation would be not something new in itself, but would be revelation about the historical situation to people in that situation, for example, the difficult crisis that the people are facing, with no resolution apparent. Revelation was that God was acting to change the situation and to change the people in that situation, so that they can act. Rather than separate certain of Jesus' sayings in themselves from the Israelite tradition that comprised an important aspect of the historical context, a relational-contextual approach attempts to discern how the text of Q or Mark references Israelite tradition in a way that provides revelation for people involved in the problematic historical situation. This suggests that the key for modern readers' understanding of Gospel materials is to become as familiar as possible with the Israelite tradition (as well as the context) out of which the historical audience (implied in the text) heard the text. Only if we as modern readers make the connection between text and metonymically signaled references to Israelite tradition can we construe the text within the range of possibilities it implies.

Gospels as Bold Declarations of a Popular Movement

Once we are aware that the popular protests and movements that came to the attention of the rulers in antiquity were only the tip of the iceberg of discontent and resistance among the people (end of chapter 2), we can recognize another aspect of Gospel materials as sources for the Jesus movement. Mark and Q appear to represent the "hidden transcript" of the Jesus movement. They are key components of communication that took place in the "sequestered sites" of communities of a movement comprised of peasants and artisans far from the surveillance of the rulers.[26] Both Mark and Q do indeed portray Jesus as boldly pronouncing God's condemnation of the rulers and their representatives to their face, in public. But these ostensibly public declarations of the people's real feelings in the face of power are components of overall "texts" performed in communities of Jesus movements.

The Gospel of Mark and the Q speeches, however, are no longer simply the usual examples of the "hidden transcript." Mark and Q bring the strongly oppositional attitudes and motivations to conscious and regular expression. By the time Mark and Q had developed toward the forms in which we have them, the activities and attitudes of the Jesus movements were well known to the Jerusalem authorities, perhaps to the Roman governors as well. A number of passages in Q and especially in Mark (and in Acts) indicate that the "subversive" Jesus movements were subject to repressive measures, arrests, and even killings. That means that the hidden transcript represented in the Gospels had indeed been publicly declared in the face of power—or that the cultivation of the hidden transcript of Gospel materials "offstage" in Jesus communities had emboldened Jesus' followers in their oppositional activities.

Mark and Q should thus be understood as intracommunity articulations of a no-longer-so-hidden mobilization of Galilean and other peasants into a village-based movement. These earliest "texts" of Gospel literature arose from a rich and deep hidden transcript of Israelite popular tradition in the interaction of the prophet Jesus and his followers in the offstage sites of Galilean and other villages. They were further developed and refined in those circumstances during the course of repeated performances in communities that, on the one hand, met out of the hearing of their rulers yet, on the other hand, knew that the latter were aware of their generally subversive agenda. These earliest "texts" of the Gospel literature are elaborate and nuanced semipublic performances of the hidden transcript. These "texts" thus empowered and emboldened those communities of the subordinate to take collective action in renewing their own community life, under the wider constraints, of course, imposed by the broader power relations determined by their rulers.

TAKING THE GOSPEL WHOLE

The implications of these considerations are, to put it succinctly, that we must "take our Gospel whole" in order to pursue a relational-contextual approach to the historical Jesus. The Gospels as whole texts provide our principal guide to the historical contextual significance of Gospel materials as communication. Far from purposely rejecting the original literary context of Gospel materials, we must rather begin with the whole story of Mark as the earliest Gospel and the Q series of Jesus-speeches focused on issues of concern to communities of Jesus' followers.[27]

The Gospel of Mark

Modern Western Christians tend to read the Gospel of Mark as a paradigmatic story of Christian discipleship. Like much else in standard interpretation of the Gospels, this has a great deal to do with modern Western individualism. Those who interpret Mark along this line, however, must do mental gymnastics in order to explain the Gospel's increasingly negative portrayal of the twelve disciples. Early in the story they are indeed individually called, constituted as the Twelve, and commissioned to extend Jesus' program of preaching and exorcism. But Peter, James, John, then all the Twelve completely misunderstand Jesus' program, want positions of power and privilege, and finally, in the climax of the story, betray, deny, and abandon Jesus.

Mark's story ends abruptly at the empty tomb as the man clothed in white directs the women to tell the disciples to proceed to Galilee, where Jesus would meet them. The readers/hearers of this open-ended story are thus invited to continue the story and the mission of Jesus back in Galilee. But Mark gives no indication that Peter and the rest of the

Twelve ever got the message, let alone acted on it. Indeed, both Paul's letter to the Galatians and the early chapters in Acts indicate that Peter and the others remained in Jerusalem, where they became the prominent "pillars" of the movement—in positions somewhat like those asked for by James and John but bluntly rejected by Jesus in Mark (10:35-45). The Gospel of Mark appears rather to be calling the movement back to its Galilean and other village roots. Mark acknowledges the Twelve as the symbolic heads of the renewed Israel, as constituted by Jesus early in the story, but clearly rejects their understanding of Jesus and his movement. The conflict between the Twelve and Jesus is at most a subplot of Mark's overall story.

If we listen in a less depoliticized way to Mark's overall story, it is evident that Jesus' primarily conflict in Mark is with the high-priestly rulers in Jerusalem and their representatives in Galilee, the scribes and Pharisees. The story comes to a climax when Jesus enters the capital city of Jerusalem and engages in one confrontation after another with the high priests and their representatives, including a demonstration against the Temple and the prophecy of its destruction. The Jerusalem rulers then arrest him, put him on trial, and turn him over to the Roman governor for crucifixion. But Mark has given clues to the outcome almost from the beginning, in the Pharisees' surveillance of Jesus and their conspiring with the Herodians to destroy him.

The dominant plot of Mark's story, therefore, must revolve around this dominant conflict. But what is Jesus doing or saying that leads the Jerusalem rulers and their representatives in Galilee to oppose and destroy him? At the beginning of the story, the scribes and Pharisees are concerned about his exorcisms (vanquishing the unclean spirits), healings, and forgiveness of sins. It might not be clear from consideration of these activities by themselves why they would be reasons for his destruction. In the context of the rest of the story as it references Israelite tradition, however, they go together (a) with Jesus' constitution of the Twelve, clearly as the representatives of the people of Israel; (b) with Jesus' sea crossings and feedings in the wilderness and further healings, clearly as the new Moses and Elijah; and (c) with his insistence on the basic commandments of God in clear appeal to the Mosaic covenant, in opposition to the scribes and Pharisees' "traditions of the elders." Jesus is unmistakably carrying out a renewal of the people of Israel, and the representatives of the Jerusalem rulers of Israel and guardians of the "great tradition" are threatened. When Jesus then enters Jerusalem and confronts the rulers, the overall plot of the Gospel becomes clear. Mark's story portrays Jesus carrying out a renewal of Israel over against (and in condemnation of) the rulers of Israel and their Roman patrons.

It may be useful to have at least a sketchy outline of the overall Markan story in mind as a frame of reference when we come to analyze particular episodes of the story in the next two chapters. (The following outline, as in the preceding analysis of the story, includes the role that Jesus plays/adapts in his mission and the movement he establishes.)

GOSPEL OF MARK AS STORY OF RENEWAL OF ISRAEL OVER AGAINST ITS RULERS

John announces coming of prophet like Moses/Elijah (1:1-13)

Jesus (as prophet) proclaims that kingdom of God is at hand (1:14-15)

Jesus (as prophet) campaigns in Galilee, healing, forgiving, and exorcising as manifestations of God's rule, and calling and constituting the Twelve as representatives of renewed Israel (1:16—3:35)

Jesus teaches mystery of kingdom in parables (4:1-34)

Jesus (as prophet) like Moses and Elijah enacting renewal of Israel in sea crossings, exorcisms, healings, wilderness feedings, and insisting on covenantal commandments (4:35—8:22/26)

Jesus (as prophet) like Moses and Elijah teaching renewed covenantal principles as criteria for entering kingdom of God, with his own suffering as positive example juxtaposed with twelve disciples as negative examples (8:22/26—10:45/52)

Jesus (as prophet) proclaims judgment of Temple, high priests (11:1—13:1-2)

Jesus' (as prophet's) speech about future exhorting solidarity and not being misled (13:3-37)

Jesus (as prophet) renews covenant, anticipating kingdom of God; is arrested and tried by high priests, then crucified by Romans (14–15)

Jesus rises and leads way to Galilee (for continuation of movement) (16:1-8)

Even from this summary outline, but especially from a reading/hearing of the whole story, it is clear that the dominant theme running throughout the Gospel is (the presence of) the kingdom of God. Most of the steps in Mark's story outlined above feature the kingdom of God stated explicitly at a key points (it is lacking only in the introductory step and the middle section focused on Jesus' actions as the new Moses/Elijah).

KINGDOM OF GOD AS THEME OF GOSPEL OF MARK

1:15—kingdom of God is at hand, theme of whole story

(3:22-27—kingdom of God is implicit, declared happening in Jesus' exorcisms)

4:11—secret of kingdom of God; plus parables of kingdom of God, 4:26, 30

9:1—kingdom of God coming in power

9:47—enter kingdom of God

10:14-15—belong to/receive kingdom of God

10:23, 24, 25—enter kingdom of God

(11:10 coming kingdom of David)

12:34—not far from kingdom of God

14:25—drink cup of renewed covenant in kingdom of God

15:43—waiting expectantly for kingdom of God

The Sequence of Jesus' Speeches Known as Q

Since Q is not a story like Mark, we cannot simply analyze its plot. Within the whole sequence of speeches in Q, however, we can discern that each speech addresses a basic concern of a community of Jesus' followers. It may help to survey the whole sequence of speeches in Q in order to gain a sense of what it is about, that is, what are the various concerns of the movement. The following outline lists the discernible speeches from the parallels in Matthew and Luke along with the apparent themes or concerns each expresses. Since it is striking how often the phrase "the kingdom of God" occurs, I also list those occurrences in parenthesis for handy reference.[28]

Q = SEQUENCE OF JESUS-SPEECHES
(WITH KINGDOM OF GOD THEME)
ADDRESSING JESUS MOVEMENT ISSUES

3:7-9, 16-17—John (as prophet) announces coming prophet to baptize with Holy Spirit and fire

6:20-49 (20)—Jesus (as prophet) announces kingdom of God as covenant renewal

7:18-35 (28)—Jesus (as successor to John) is indeed coming prophet bringing renewal = kingdom of God

9:57—10:16 (9:60, 62; 10:9, 11)—Jesus sends envoys to heal and curse = kingdom of God as renewal and judgment

11:2-4, 9-13 (2)—prayer for kingdom of God, which is renewal, but with testing

11:14-20 (20)—Jesus' (as prophet's) exorcisms = manifestations of kingdom of God (implied judgment of critics)

11:29-32—Jesus (as prophet) declares something greater than Jonah or Solomon is here

11:39-52—Jesus (as prophet) utters woes against Pharisees

12:2-12—Jesus exhorts bold confession when hauled before authorities

12:22-31 (31)—Jesus reassures that subsistence materializes in single-minded pursuit of kingdom of God

12:49-59—Jesus' (as prophet's) fiery mission (crisis) means divisions, but resolves conflicts

13:18-21 (18, 20)—Jesus (as prophet) declares two kingdom of God parables

13:28-29, 34-35 + 14:16-24 (29)—Jesus (as prophet) pronounces kingdom of God banquet, both positive and judgmental

16:16—Jesus (as prophet) says kingdom of God suffers violence

17:22-37—Jesus (as prophet) warns of day of Son of Man = judgment positive and negative

22:28-30 (30)—Jesus (as prophet) constitutes twelve representatives realizing justice for Israel in banquet of kingdom of God

It seems clear that the theme of the sequence of speeches that comprise Q is the kingdom of God. Moreover, closer inspection of the issues or concerns of the individual speeches suggests that the overall concern of

Q and the concrete meaning or program of "the kingdom of God" is the renewal of Israel. The "kingdom of God" phrase occurs fourteen times at key points in ten out of the sixteen speeches delineated above. In these Jesus-speeches in Q, further, the kingdom of God has remarkably concrete economic, social, and political references. In the long opening speech, Jesus promises the kingdom of God to the poor and hungry. In the Lord's Prayer the kingdom of God means sufficient food for hungry people and cancellation of debts. In the exhortation not to be anxious, single-minded pursuit of the kingdom will result in sufficient nourishment and adequate shelter. In the kingdom of God, people will be banqueting with the ancestors. In response to John's question about whether Jesus is indeed the coming prophet, the kingdom is associated with the overcoming of despair, despondency, and disease. In response to the charge of possession by Beelzebul, Jesus declares that his exorcisms of demons are manifestations of the victory of God's kingdom over Satan's. In the mission speech Jesus commissions envoys to preach the kingdom and heal people. In the closing speech Jesus declares that the twelve representatives of Israel will be effecting justice for the people. This all adds up to a social and economic renewal of family and community life in the villages that constitute Israel. Many of the Q speeches portray Jesus as a prophet, whether pronouncing prophetic oracles of God's judgment on Jerusalem and woes against the Pharisees, or performing the actions of a prophet who is indeed bringing restoration of life in the power of the Spirit. As we shall explore further, Jesus as a new Moses enacts a covenant renewal (6:20–49) and as the new Elijah sends out envoys (9:57—10:16).

While Mark's story and Q's speeches have somewhat different emphases, their respective representations of Jesus have a remarkably similar agenda. Mark focuses more on the healings and exorcisms as parts of a wider program of renewal of the people of Israel vividly reminiscent of Moses and Elijah, the founding and renewing prophets of Israel, respectively. While Mark includes a strong statement of economic sufficiency along with a warning against economic exploitation and political domination, economic sufficiency for a poor and hungry people is more prominent, even dominant, in the Q speeches. On the other hand, Mark includes more condemnations of the Jerusalem rulers and their representatives and their Roman sponsors for their religio-economic oppression and their religio-political repression of the people. The kingdom of

God theme declared at the outset of Mark's story seems more integral in the Q speeches. With these somewhat different emphases, however, the overall program of Jesus' prophetic teaching and practice is clearly the renewal of Israel in both Mark and Q.

It is significant to note, finally, that insofar as the dominant plot of the Gospel has two complementary aspects, the renewal of Israel and the condemnation of the rulers, so the kingdom of God as the dominant theme of Mark has two aspects. The counterpart of the renewal of Israel as the realization of the kingdom of God is the judgment of the oppressive rulers of Israel by the kingly rule of God. Although God's condemnation of the rulers may not seem as prominent in the Q sequence of speeches as in Mark's Gospel, the particular speeches that pronounce the judgment or exclusion of the rulers explicitly link that judgment with the coming/presence of the kingdom of God. The kingdom of God is the overarching theme that encompasses Jesus' prophetic condemnation of oppressive rulers as well as his prophetic renewal of Israel—the subjects of the next two chapters.

GOD'S JUDGMENT
OF THE ROMAN IMPERIAL ORDER

> *Judas the Gaulanite [a teacher] and Saddok the Pharisee launched a rebellion. They said that the tribute amounted to downright slavery and appealed to the people to seek their independence, . . . saying that God would aid them until their endeavor succeeded. . . . They agree in all other respects with the views of the Pharisees, except that they have an unconquerable passion for freedom, since they are convinced that God is their exclusive ruler and master.*
>
> —Josephus

> *Some Pharisees and Herodians, to entrap him, . . . asked: "Is it lawful to pay tribute to Caesar or not?" . . . Jesus said to them, "Give to Caesar the things that belong to Caesar, and to God the things that belong to God."*
>
> —Mark 12:13-17

Once we "take the Gospel whole," it is clear not only that Jesus spearheaded a program of renewal of the people. He also pronounced God's judgment on the people's rulers, on the Romans themselves as well as on their Jerusalem rulers, the face that the Roman imperial order presented to the people of Palestine.

In the Q speeches Jesus offers the kingdom of God to the poor, for whom it means sufficient food and cancellation of debts as well as mutual sharing and cooperation and personal healing (Q 6:20-49; 7:18-35; 11:2-4). The kingdom of God that brings renewal for the people, however, utterly excludes the people's rulers and places them under God's judgment. The coming prophet will "baptize" with the fire of judgment as well as the Spirit of renewal (3:7-9). The speech that touts the personal healing now happening in Jesus' prophetic activities also places Antipas, in his fine clothing and fancy palace, outside the purview of

Jesus' mission and the kingdom of God (7:18-35). Those who presume, on the basis of their distinguished lineage from Abraham, that they are "the sons of the kingdom" (i.e., apparently the Jerusalem elite) will find themselves excluded from the future banquet of the kingdom (3:16-17; 13:28-29). Indeed, in a traditional prophetic lament Jesus proclaims that the ruling house of Jerusalem has already been condemned by God (13:34-35).

Similarly in the Gospel of Mark, after conducting a mission of personal and community renewal among Galilean and other villagers, Jesus marches up to Jerusalem, where he engages in a dramatic confrontation with the high priests, scribes, and elders that leads to his arrest, trial, and crucifixion. Along the way he proclaims not only that the kingdom of God is ready for the people to "receive" and "enter," but also that it is impossible for the wealthy to enter the kingdom (10:13-16, 17-25). Moreover, Mark's story includes indications that, in the coming of the kingdom with Jesus' program of exorcism, healing, and community solidarity, God is also overcoming the rule of Rome, as we shall explore below. In both of our earliest Gospel documents taken in their integrity, therefore, the kingdom as renewal of the people and judgment of the rulers go together.

Recent liberal interpreters of Jesus are clearly uncomfortable with the judgmental side of Jesus' mission (as noted in the introduction). This is a dramatic departure from the earlier view made popular mainly by Albert Schweitzer of Jesus as an "apocalyptic" prophet who preached the end of the world. To modern Western sensitivities, however, the apocalyptic Jesus seems perilously close to being a deluded fanatic, since his predictions of a presumed "cosmic catastrophe" proved false. Some recent American interpreters have avoided this embarrassing conclusion by rejecting as secondary any of Jesus' sayings that might seem "apocalyptic" in tone or motif. This makes Jesus into an utterly unique historical figure—a historical impossibility, of course—different from both his Jewish contemporaries before him and his own followers after him.

Both the earlier picture of Jesus as an apocalyptic preacher and the more recent attempt to eliminate apocalyptic elements are rooted in the modern scholarly construct of "apocalyptic," which is highly problematic.[1] It is questionable whether this synthetic modern scholarly construct is applicable to any particular ancient Jewish text, including those classified in the genre of "apocalypse." More particularly, once we are more sensitive to metaphoric language and hyperbole, it is difficult to find any ancient Judean texts that attest belief in "the end of the world" or a "cosmic catastrophe." We need to abandon the modern concept of "apocalyptic" and take a fresh look at the way the earliest Gospel documents portray Jesus' pronouncement of judgment. Far from isolating the judgmental elements from their context in Mark's overall story and the series of speeches in Q, we must consider how Jesus' pronouncement of judgment against rulers draws on a broader pattern deeply rooted in ancient Israelite tradition.

THE CONDITIONS OF RENEWAL: JUDGMENT OF RULERS

A Basic Pattern in Israelite Tradition

Israelite cultural tradition, as known primarily through the Hebrew Bible, features a fundamental pattern in which the liberation or restoration of the people entails God's defeat or judgment of Israel's foreign or domestic rulers. The classic case is the story of the exodus from bondage to Pharaoh in Egypt. The pattern is explicit in the earliest Hebrew poems, the Song of Miriam and the Song of Deborah (Exod 15:1-18; Judges 5, respectively). In "classical" prophetic oracles, which focus on God's indictment and sentence of kings and their officers, the point of judgment is to alleviate the oppression and suffering of the people. This pattern is rooted in the structure and dynamics of the situation in which kings exploit and oppress the people and refuse to listen to appeals to free the people or to prophetic pronouncements against their oppression. God's action against rulers is necessary for the independence of or justice for the people.

This pattern continues in literature produced by scribal circles, clearly in response to the Seleucid (successors of Alexander the Great) imperial regime's tightening oppression of the Judean people and attempts to suppress the traditional covenantal way of life. God is portrayed as finally asserting ultimate rule over history in two complementary actions: judgment of the oppressive foreign empire and restoration of the people, the first obviously necessary to make the second possible.

The example best known to ancient Judeans as well as to modern readers is the vision of beastly empires in Daniel 7. "An Ancient One took his throne, . . . the court sat in judgment." Then "the beast was put to death . . . and given over to be burned with fire." Finally "one like a son of man" was "given dominion and glory and kingship" forever by the Ancient One. This is interpreted to mean that the oppressive last empire, which attacked God's people and their Law, would have its dominion "totally destroyed," whereupon "the kingship and dominion shall be given to the people of the holy ones of the Most High" (Dan 7:9-14, 23-27). A similar pattern forms the basic agenda of other visions in Daniel 8–12 and of the Apocalypse of Weeks and the Apocalypse of Animals in the book of *1 Enoch*. In another document completed under Roman rule the whole scenario of God's finally coming "to work vengeance on the nations" so that "Israel will be happy" unfolds even more explicitly as the implementation of the kingdom of God: "Then his kingdom will appear throughout his whole creation" (*Testament of Moses* 10:1, 7-10).[2]

In *Psalms of Solomon* 17 the same agenda of God's final assertion of ultimate sovereignty in history is implemented by an "anointed son of David" as God's agent. The situation is again Israel's subjection by empire, in this case clearly the Romans under Pompey. The singers of the psalm appeal to God to raise up "the son of David" and give him strength "to destroy unrighteous rulers who trample down Jerusalem, . . . to destroy them with the word of his mouth." He will then "gather a holy people, . . . lead them in justice, . . . and distribute them upon the land according to their tribes" (17:21-28). The whole psalm begins and ends with the acclamation that the Lord is king forevermore.

This brief survey indicates that the expectation was widespread, at least in scribal-scholarly circles, that, in their situation of oppression by foreign empire(s), God would intervene in the near future to judge the empire and to restore the people to independence or sovereignty (and vindicate the martyrs). In several texts, moreover, this double action of God is represented as "the kingdom of God."

It is evident, therefore, that when we find Mark and Q representing Jesus in a dual program of mediating God's renewal of Israel and pronouncing God's judgment against rulers, as two sides of the coming of the kingdom of God, this is a particular adaptation of a common pattern deeply rooted in Israelite culture and still current in Roman times. It is all the more striking that this pattern is evident both in the overall structure of Mark and Q and in particular statements in each (see esp. Mark 3:22-28; 10:13-16, 17-25; Q 3:16-17; 13:28-29).

A brief comparison with *Psalms of Solomon* 17 also reveals the difference between Jesus' understanding of the kingdom of God and that of a scribal group. The scribal composers of this psalm, from their position in the city of Jerusalem, are concerned for the sanctity of the holy city and anticipate an imperial yet scribal-style "anointed one, son of David," in fulfillment of the Davidic covenant articulated in the Jerusalem "great tradition" of 2 Samuel 7.[3] Jesus, on the other hand (as we shall see below), speaking and acting in both Mark and Q from the popular tradition and perspective of Galilean villagers, includes the Jerusalem elite among the "unrighteous rulers" whom God will judge.[4] This brief survey of a deeply rooted Israelite cultural pattern indicates that he was in tune with widespread and long-standing anti-imperial currents in ancient Palestine.

Further Opposition to Rulers in Israelite Tradition

Israelite tradition is rich with condemnation of oppressive rulers above and beyond the basic pattern of God's judgment of rulers in order to restore the people. Much of the heritage of opposition to foreign rulers derived originally from the Israelite peasantry (see early traditions now included in Exodus 1–15; Joshua 2–12; Judges 3–12). The Mosaic covenant that comprised the principles of self-governance of the people understood God as the exclusive king of the people, thus excluding human kings (e.g., Exodus 20; Joshua 24; Judg 8:22; 1 Sam 8:1-6).

Following Solomon's establishment of an imperial kingship in Jerusalem and his construction of the original Temple by imposing "forced labor" on "all Israel" (1 Kgs 5:13-18), the ten northern tribes rebelled against the Davidic monarchy in Jerusalem (1 Kgs 12:1-20). This rebellion of most of Israel from Jerusalem's domination would presumably have been remembered among Israelite descendants in the north, particularly after the Hasmoneans again asserted Jerusalem rule over Samaria and Galilee just a hundred years before the birth of Jesus. The paradigmatic northern Israelite prophets Elijah and Elisha led popular movements against Ahab and Jezebel's attempts to consolidate power in a permanent capital. The prophets Amos, Micah, and Isaiah all pronounced oracles against the service of God(s) in temples as well as against the kings' and their officers' oppression of the peasantry. Most dramatically, perhaps, Jeremiah pronounced God's condemnation of both the Jerusalem Temple and the monarchy because the whole political–economic–religious system violated the principles of the Mosaic covenant (Jeremiah 7; 26; 22:13-19).

From the outset of the Persian-sponsored restoration of the Temple and high priesthood in Jerusalem there appears to have been widespread opposition (Isaiah 56–66; Malachi). Contrary to previous claims, moreover, Judean apocalyptic literature attests to a future destruction of the Temple, but not a rebuilding of the Temple.[5] The priestly-scribal community that launched a new exodus to Qumran where they formed a renewed Mosaic covenant community was building on long-standing opposition to incumbent high priesthoods.

Much of the same Judean literature that indicates opposition to the Temple or at least to the incumbent high priesthood also gives vivid expression to the strong currents of resistance directed against imperial rule that emerged in scribal circles in the centuries prior to Jesus and his contemporaries. The Maccabean Revolt against the Seleucid imperial forces indicates that the anti-imperial currents were also strong among the people. Both scribal circles and the peasantry would have been drawing on the long Israelite tradition of resistance to foreign rule (summarized in chapter 2).

Most intriguing, since the discovery of the Dead Sea Scrolls we know that the scribal-priestly community at Qumran articulated a worldview that combined an explanation for the people's situation of subjection to alien forces and a scenario for future liberation. According to its "Community Rule" (1QS) two opposing superhuman spirits, of Light and of Darkness, were ruling over history until the time of God's "visitation," at which time the power of Darkness would be overcome and the original conditions of creation restored. According to its "War Scroll" (1QM), moreover, at some point in the near future the community itself would join the forces of Light in successful battle against the "Kittim," that is, the Romans, and the forces of Darkness. Although this dualistic worldview mystifies the concrete imperial causes of the people's oppression, by viewing the imperial forces as working under the sway of Belial and therefore hopelessly out of control until the time of visitation, the community avoided any suicidal outbursts against the Roman forces that would simply annihilate them in retaliation. Insofar as the Qumranites themselves had formed a mutually supportive and rigorously disciplined community of solidarity in the power of the Prince of Light, they themselves were not under the power of Darkness, at least in their community life; that is, they themselves were not individually or collectively possessed by demonic forces.

Conditions of Social Conflict under Roman Rule in Palestine

The way in which Roman imperial rule operated in Galilee and Judea seriously exacerbated the conditions of social conflict, as summarized in the previous chapters. We can recapitulate the principal points that more directly affected the emergence of Jesus and his movement (sketched in chapters 1–3). Although Roman imperial rule was mostly mediated through Herodian kingship and the Judean high priesthood, Roman imperial practice did affect the conditions in which Jesus' mission and movement emerged more directly as well.

The Roman imposition of Herodian client kingship in Palestine, and Herod's retention of the temple-state, meant that the people now had multiple layers of rulers with their demands of taxes or tribute on top of tithes and offerings. Herod's massive development projects and gifts to the imperial family and foreign cities would have placed a further burden on the peasantry, who formed his principal economic base. His cultural innovations, moreover, would have compounded the fundamental structural conflict. His building of cities and temples to Caesar, his total rebuilding of the Jerusalem Temple in grand Hellenistic-Roman style as one of the wonders of the world, and his installation into the high priesthood of figures from the Jewish diaspora who had no previous contact with the people would have further alienated the people.

Galileans, who had only recently come under Jerusalem rule, would likely have had a great deal of ambivalence about the Temple and high priesthood, to whom they had not previously owed tithes and other dues. Moreover, the peasantry of Galilee had borne the brunt of repeated Roman conquests of Palestine, with major massacres in the areas of Nazareth and Magdala (and Capernaum). The Roman imposition of Herod Antipas as a ruler who for the first time in history lived directly in Galilee surely meant an unprecedented rigor in the collection of taxes. His ambitious construction of two capital cities within two decades meant an unusual economic drain on the Galilean peasantry precisely during the lifetime of Jesus and those who would join his movement. Further, to the Galileans the Roman-style cities Antipas built with such revenues were constant reminders of Roman imperial rule.

It is not surprising that popular protest and resistance erupted with increasing frequency precisely during the lifetime of Jesus and his followers. The popular messianic movements in Galilee and Judea attempted to establish the people's independence of both Jerusalem and Roman rule. Radical Pharisees and other teachers spearheaded a refusal to render the Roman tribute, claiming that God was their true and only Lord and Master. Popular prophets led movements anticipating, among other things, the collapse of high-priestly and Roman rule in Jerusalem, along with the walls of the city.

It has to be striking that Jesus' mission and movement are framed historically between these popular movements that took distinctively Israelite form. All of these movements indicate that those distinctive Israelite traditions of popular resistance and independence were very much alive in Judea and Galilee at the time of Jesus. The distinctive social forms of these movements clearly prefigure Jesus and his movement.

The Israelite tradition of opposition to oppressive rulers and the conditions of endemic social conflict exacerbated by Roman rule suggest that the people whom Jesus addressed would have expected and welcomed a condemnation of the high priests, perhaps of the Temple itself, as well as of Roman rule. Was Jesus somehow totally different from other popular leaders and movements and dissident scribal circles? Or was he distinctive mainly in the particular mode of his pronouncement of God's judgment against the Roman imperial order?

JESUS' PROPHETIC CONDEMNATION OF THE TEMPLE AND HIGH PRIESTS

The face that Roman imperial rule presented in Palestine was that of its client rulers, the Herodian "tetrarch" Antipas in Galilee and in Judea the high priests based in the Temple in Jerusalem. The Temple and high priesthood were also traditionally the ruling institutions of Israel. A prophetic program of God's judgment against the imperial order in order to advance the renewal of the people of Israel would, in the first instance, have to focus on the Roman client rulers of Israel, the high priesthood based in the Temple.

Prophetic Pronouncement of God's Judgment of the Jerusalem Rulers in Q

The sequence of speeches in Q begins with John the Baptizer's announcement that a prophet is coming who will baptize both with Spirit (constructive renewal) and with fire (destructive judgment; 3:7-9, 16-17). It concludes with Jesus' declaration that the Twelve, as representatives of the people, are to sit on twelve seats in the kingdom establishing justice for the tribes of Israel (6:20-49; 10:2-16; 22:28-30). The disappearance of the actual rulers of Israel (Roman, Herodian, Jerusalem?) so that the Twelve can function as representative leaders appears to be the focus of the Q speech that incorporated, in some way, the two prophetic statements of 13:28-29 and 34-35 and the parable in 14:16-24.[6] Moreover, each of the three steps in the speech and the speech as a whole combine God's judgment of rulers with God's deliverance of the people that we found in the fundamental Israelite pattern examined above. After the second step in the speech explains the reason for God's judgment announced in the first, the third step repeats in parable form the basic message of the first step.

> [Many] shall come from the east and west
> and recline with Abraham and Isaac and Jacob in the kingdom (of God).
> {And the sons of the kingdom} will be cast out,
> and there will be weeping and gnashing of teeth. (Q 13:28-29)[7]

Recent studies of Q have tended to read 13:28-29 from a later Christian viewpoint of God's rejection of Jews in favor of Gentiles. They take the "many coming from east and west" as a reference to Gentiles and "the sons of the kingdom/you" as a reference to "the Jews." Indeed, that is the way Matthew and Luke used this Q material, following the Roman destruction of Jerusalem and in light of the "mission to the Gentiles" that both of them feature. One of the cardinal principles for interpretation of Q, however, is to distinguish the material's significance in Q from its later use by Matthew and Luke. Other than this reading of this passage, Q speeches contain no indication of any "Gentile mission" and know nothing of the actual destruction of Jerusalem.

There is virtually no comparative textual basis, moreover, for concluding that the "many coming from east and west" are Gentiles. The rich "parallels" to such language from Israelite prophets and Judean scribal literature all refer rather to the ingathering of dispersed Israelites at the time of the future restoration of Israel (Zech 2:10; 8:7-8; Isa 42:5-6; Bar 4:4; 5:5; *1 Enoch* 57:1; *Ps. Sol.* 11:2-3).[8] The image in Q 13:28-29 is thus clearly that of Israel being gathered in, for the banquet of the kingdom of God, another common image of the restoration of Israel in the prophets (Isa 55:1; Jer 31:7-14).

Another principle of interpretation for Q is to look for links and common images across the various speeches that comprise the work. Abraham's appearance (with Isaac and Jacob) in Q 13:28-29 is anticipated by his appearance in John the Baptizer's opening harangue in 3:7-9: "Bear fruits worthy of repentance, and do not start saying to yourselves, 'We have Abraham as our father'; for I tell you, God is able from these stones to raise up children to Abraham." Again because Q focuses the mission in Israel, and lacks a mission to "the Gentiles," it is evident that John is not here haranguing "the Jews," but rather some group within Israel. Those who would have boasted of their proper lineage from Abraham would have to have been the aristocracy in Jerusalem. This rhetorical reference to Abraham in 3:7-9 is the key to hearing the parallel rhetorical reference to Abraham, Isaac, and Jacob in 13:28-29. There "the sons of the kingdom" must refer to those who presumed that (especially) they were the heirs of the kingdom because they were the descendants of Abraham, Isaac, and Jacob.[9] But in 3:16-17 John had already warned that God could raise up children from the stones! The statement in 13:28-29 is thus a double-edged prophecy of the banquet of the kingdom. But the principal thrust of the statement was the exclusion of the elite, who would be "weeping and gnashing their teeth."[10]

The second step in the speech is almost verbatim in Matthew's and Luke's parallel texts. The oral composition is almost palpable: after the mournful repetitive address come two parallel lines (of two stresses each) with parallel sounds and ideas, followed by two four-stress lines that articulate an analogy between God and a mother hen, ending with a purposely brief two-stress line that uses the same verb for Jerusalem's refusal as for God's will.

> O Jerusalem, Jerusalem!
> You kill the prophets
> and stone those sent to you.
> How often would I have gathered your children together
> As a hen gathers her brood under her wings,
> And you refused.
> Behold your house is forsaken!
> For I tell you:
> You will not see me until you say:
> "Blessed is he who comes in the name of the Lord." (Q 13:34-35)

In form this statement is a prophetic lament in which the prophet speaks as the mouthpiece of God. It both assumes and announces that the city lamented is already destroyed in anticipation of God's imminent judgment. Jesus' performance of God's lament over the desolation of Jerusalem references Israelite tradition in richly interconnected ways. In form it reminds the hearer of previous prophetic lamentation, such as that in Amos (5:2-3): "Fallen, no more to rise is the maiden Israel; forsaken on her land with no one to raise her up."

In such prophetic pronouncements God's lamentation anticipates that of the ruling city when the judgment is finally executed: "Therefore thus says the Lord, the God of hosts, the Lord: In all the squares there shall be wailing; and in all the streets they shall say 'Alas! alas!' They shall call . . . those skilled in lamentation, to wailing" (Amos 5:16-17).

That the tradition of prophetic laments was still very much alive in first-century Palestine is evident from the persistent pronouncement (for seven years) by the peasant prophet Jesus ben Hananiah just prior to the great revolt. Standing in the Temple he cried:

> A voice from the east,
> A voice from the west,
> A voice from the four winds:
> A voice against Jerusalem and the temple!
> A voice against bridegrooms and brides!
> A voice against the whole people! (Josephus, *War* 6.300–309)

Further, Jesus of Nazareth's indictment of the Jerusalem ruling house for "killing the prophets" resonates with a long Israelite tradition.

Not always, but often enough, the rulers had killed prophets. Ahab and Jezebel had sent death squads out to assassinate Elijah, that "troubler of Israel" (1 Kings 19; 18:17). At the time of Jeremiah, King Jehoiakim had similarly sent agents to Egypt to hunt down and kill the prophet Uriah son of Shemiah, who had fled there for refuge. Temple officials tried to lynch Jeremiah himself after his prophecy of God's condemnation of the Temple (Jer 26:7-23). This tradition would have been in the forefront of people's minds around the time of Jesus because both Roman governors and their client rulers in Palestine killed several prophets. Most vivid in the memories of Jesus' followers, Herod Antipas had arrested and beheaded John the Baptizer for his insistence on covenantal justice (Josephus, *Ant.* 18.116–19; cf. Mark 6:17-29).[11]

The image of God wanting to gather the children as a hen gathers her brood under her wing resonates with, even as it adapts in folksy fashion, the traditional image from the Song of Moses, where God is "like an eagle that stirs up its nest and hovers over its young, spreading its wings" (Deut 32:11). The Song of Moses, which likely would still have been widely used, celebrated God's original exodus liberation and covenantal formation of Israel as his own special people. "Children" (or "daughters") was a standing image for the villages subject to a mother city (as in Isa 51:17-18). Jesus'/God's lament in Q 13:34-35 therefore, in a rustic adaptation of the traditional representation of God as a warrior-like eagle, portrayed God in a more earthy and caring maternal manner as a mother hen attempting to protect her young from the predatory Jerusalem rulers.

The last line of the lament in Q 13:34-35, finally, recites a key line from Psalm 118. Since this psalm was sung at festival time, particularly Passover, it would have been very familiar to Jesus' hearers. It was a thanksgiving hymn for previous deliverance and an appeal for future salvation: "Hosanna! Deliver us!" As part of God's/Jesus' lament, he wails that the Jerusalem rulers would not see God until they welcomed "the one who comes in the name of the Lord," that is, Jesus in Q. But of course they never would do that. Indeed, they had killed the latest prophet sent by God, the Jesus who speaks in this prophetic lament. Since they refused/forsook God, they are about to be refused/forsaken by God.

The prophetic lament in Q 13:34-35 thus fits well with the prophetic statement in 13:28-29. In the prophecy of the final gathering of Israel in the banquet of the kingdom, those who presumed that, as the proper descendants of the founding patriarchs, they were the prime heirs of the kingdom, were excluded. The prophetic lament in 13:34-35, identifying them explicitly as the Jerusalem ruling house, mockingly mourns their future desolation in God's judgment due to their refusal to hear God's repeated warnings.

The parable of the banquet in Q 14:16-24 forms a fitting sequel and conclusion to the two prophetic statements of 13:28-29 and 34-35. The banquet metaphor in the parable picks up the theme of the banquet of the kingdom, that is, the gathering and restoration of Israel, from 13:28-29. A "great banquet" also evokes images of the wealthy and powerful elite. Indeed, the invited guests turn out to be wealthy men who, in utter contrast to subsistence peasants, buy additional fields and multiple yoke of oxen to plow them (the Lukan version must be closer to Q, and is paralleled by the version in *Gospel of Thomas* 64; Matthew has recast the story as about a king's wedding banquet). These wealthy invited guests refuse to come to the banquet, whereupon "the poor, the maimed, the blind, and the lame" are gathered in. The parable thus clearly evokes the analogy of the self-exclusion of the elite, and that parallels the same motif in the prophetic lament in Q 13:34-35. The final statement in the parable, in 14:24, parallels the exclusion of the presumptuous elite in 13:28-29: "I tell you, none of those men who were invited shall taste my banquet." If we are attentive hearers, remembering previous speeches in the Q sequence, the poor and blind and lame invited from the alleys are the same people who were offered the kingdom and given new life in 6:20 and 7:22.

Demonstration and Prophecies against the Temple and High Priests in Mark

From the outset of Mark's story it is evident that the prophet Jesus' renewal of Israel stands in sharp opposition to the Jerusalem high priests and their Roman imperial sponsors.[12] Indeed, early in the narrative Jesus' program of healing and exorcism has become so threatening that the Pharisees and Herodians plot to destroy him (3:1-5). Once Jesus has marched into Jerusalem, he carries out a disruptive prophetic demonstration in the Temple (11:15-17; cf. 11:12-24), and then engages in a series of condemnations of the Temple, the high priests, and the scribes, after which he announces the destruction of the Temple (11:27—13:2).

Thereupon the high priests and scribes form a surreptitious plot, arrest Jesus, accuse him of threatening to destroy the Temple and to build another in three days (14:1-2, 53-64, esp. 58), and turn him over to the Roman governor for crucifixion, during which he is again accused of having threatened to destroy the Temple (15:29). It is difficult to imagine how Mark could have presented a stronger portrayal of Jesus' opposition to and condemnation of the Temple and high priests.[13]

Mark (11:15-17) portrays Jesus' demonstration in the Temple as forcible if not violent, with Jesus physically "overturning tables of the money changers" and "not allowing anyone to carry anything through the temple [courtyard]." He was effectively blocking the normal operations integral to (not corruptions of!) the functioning of the religious political-economy of the Temple, such as money changing and the selling of doves.[14]

In interpretation of his disruptive action, Jesus recites a "prophecy" that is unidentified in Mark's narrative. In the retrospect we enjoy, of canonized prophetic books, this prophecy appears to be a combination of a line from Isaiah (56:7) with one from Jeremiah (7:11). This almost certainly indicates that the prophecy was being recited from popular tradition (not a written scroll). The second line, "you have made it a bandits' den," would have been an unmistakable reference to Jeremiah's famous prophecy against the original Temple in Jerusalem (7:1-15). Jeremiah had prophesied that God had condemned the original Temple because its officials were stealing from the people, in violation of the Mosaic covenant commandments, and then presuming to use the Temple (where they believed God would keep them secure) as their hideout, their bandits' den. The first line of Jesus' prophetic statement, "my house shall be called a house of prayer for all peoples," as indicated by its original context in Isaiah 56, was part of a prophetic appeal to make the (second) Temple a center where God could gather the outcasts of Israel and other peoples (Isa 56:8).

Jesus' dramatic disruption of Temple business was also a symbolic prophetic demonstration. Isaiah had gone barefoot and naked for three years to enact symbolically the prophecy that the Assyrian Empire would lead away Egyptians (to whom the Judean monarchy was looking for defense) as captives (Isaiah 20). Jeremiah had worn an ox yoke on his neck around Jerusalem to dramatize God's demand that the Judean monarchy submit to the yoke of the Babylonian emperor (Jeremiah 27–28). Refer-

encing this tradition of prophetic demonstrations, Jesus was thus symbolically acting out a new prophetic condemnation not just of the building but of the Temple system, because of its oppression of the people, as
indicated in the reference to Jeremiah's original condemnation of the
Temple system. The high priests and scribes knew what Jesus had just
done: from this point "they kept looking for a way to kill him," just as the
earlier officers of the Temple sought to lynch Jeremiah after his oracle
pronouncing God's judgment against the Temple (Jeremiah 26).

That the point of Jesus' action is indeed that God is about to destroy
the Temple is confirmed from the way the Markan narrative frames the
demonstration. Just prior to the demonstration in the Temple, Jesus,
not finding any fruit on a fig tree, pronounced a curse on the tree: "May
no one ever eat fruit from you again" (11:12-14). Then immediately
after his demonstration against the Temple, when Peter points out that
"the fig tree you cursed has withered," Jesus makes an ominous declaration: "Have faith in God. Truly I tell you, if you say to this mountain,
'Be taken up and thrown into the sea,' and . . . believe that what you say
will come to pass, it will be done for you" (11:20-24). Jesus is (still) referring to the mount on which the Temple stood. One can trust God:
the Temple will be removed/destroyed.

After Jesus turns the high priests', scribes', and elders' question
about the source of his authority/power into their tacit admission that
they themselves have no authority/power among the people (11:27-32),
he tells the parable of the tenants of a vineyard (12:1-9).[15] Developed as
it is with several allegorical twists (e.g., "a beloved son," which must allude to Jesus; cf. Mark 1:11; 9:7), it works as a parable told to and directed against the ruling aristocracy. To hear this parable, however, we
must again remove some of the Christian theological wax from our ears.
The high priests are hardly "Jewish leaders." Mark has just demonstrated that they have no authority whatever among the people as leaders. Neither in this episode nor in Mark as a whole is there any
suggestion of the replacement of "Judaism" by "Christianity." Mark
has Jesus direct the parable in 12:1-8 and the rhetorical question in 12:9
pointedly at the high priests, scribes, and elders (11:27; 12:12). Moreover, they immediately recognize that they are implicated and resolve to
arrest Jesus, but are afraid of the crowd. Here, as throughout Mark's
story, the fundamental conflict lies between rulers and ruled, not "Judaism" and "Christianity."

Like Jesus' prophetic demonstration against the Temple, this parable vibrates with Israelite prophetic tradition. It opens with a vivid reference to a famous and familiar prophecy and prophetic image (Ps 80:8-13; Jer 2:21; 12:10; Ezek 15:1-6; 19:10; Hos 10:1). In the most famous, Isaiah 5, God had sung a "love song" about a vineyard that turned into a prophetic condemnation of those (obviously the ruling elite) who "added field to field" in their oppression of the indebted peasantry. In the parable of the tenants Jesus thus adapts a traditional prophetic image of the vineyard of which God was the owner. Jesus' parable sharpens the focus, zeroing in on the tenants of the vineyard. Far from delivering the fruits of justice (the point in Isaiah's love song/prophecy), they (the priestly rulers of Jerusalem) had even treated God's servants with violence. Obviously the master of the vineyard would not stand idly by. God was coming to destroy the priestly tenants and to give the vineyard to others.

Although the parable of the tenants is told *against* the Jerusalem rulers, it is only ostensibly told *to* them. Like the Gospel story as a whole, the parable of the master of the vineyard and the tenants was recited to the people, in particular those in the Jesus movement, primarily villagers in Galilee and beyond. The parable would have resonated with these "others" in their historical context in ways that deserve some further attention. Galilean and Judean peasants were very familiar with the political-economic relations represented in the parable. Archaeological excavations have confirmed that from the time of Herod, at least, high-priestly as well as Herodian families had steadily built up large estates farmed by tenants who were expected to deliver the produce to their absentee landowners, who had built themselves lavish mansions in Jerusalem.[16] Such estates were created by foreclosing on the loans made by the wealthy to heavily indebted peasants, who were then transformed into sharecroppers.[17] In Galilee as well, absentee landlords (probably Herodian officers) began taking advantage of the increasing pressures on the peasantry under the tightened administration of Herod Antipas to take control of their land, although the process was surely not yet as far along as in Judea and in the "royal estates" in the Great Plain just to the south of Galilee. Peasants knew very well that many of their number were being transformed from freeholders farming their own ancestral lands into tenants of the wealthy rulers and their officers who had taken effective control (ownership?) of those lands. That, of course, was in direct contradiction to Mosaic covenantal laws (e.g., prohibition of interest and cancellation of debts) and prophetic traditions (e.g., the Naboth's vineyard story and Elijah's prophecy in 1 Kings 19)!

Jesus' followers and other peasants would thus have sympathized with the behavior of the tenants, who they would have understood as just trying to reassert claims to what was rightfully theirs in the first place, as confirmed by the traditional Mosaic covenantal provisions of prohibition of interest on loans and of seventh-year cancellation of debts. Yet they also knew well that they dared not risk acting on their resentments lest their powerful absentee landlords take retaliatory action to destroy them. Palestinian peasants had firsthand knowledge of the slice of life portrayed in the parable of the tenants. They would have felt vindicated to hear this story clearly signaling that God would take action against the predatory priestly rulers of Israel, the tenants of God's vineyard, and give the vineyard to others—that is, give it back to its rightful heirs, the peasant families to whom it had been given as an inheritance in the first place. The peasant hearers in the crowd would have related to the parable only after they recognized its application, that is, once they recognized that the devious and violent tenants were the Jerusalem elite.

After his prolonged confrontation with the high priests and other groups that shared power in Jerusalem, Jesus announces to four of the Twelve that "these great buildings" will be destroyed (13:1-2). Because Mark's story is usually read in sections and fragments, partly influenced by its division into chapters and verses, rather than as a whole story, this prophecy of Jesus is often read only in connection with the rest of the "little apocalypse" in chapter 13. Jesus' long discourse about the future (13:5-37), however, is introduced not by 13:1-2 but by the question it occasions in 13:3-4 ("when will this be . . . ?"). Jesus' announcement of the destruction of the Temple (or Jerusalem) in 13:1-2, contrary to previous "readings," rather functions in the overall story as the completion of the confrontation between Jesus and the ruling groups that is set up by his entry into Jerusalem and begins with the demonstration against the Temple. After acting out or pronouncing God's condemnation of Temple, high priests, Sadducees, and scribes, Jesus announces that the Temple (or Jerusalem as a whole), the basis of their power, is to be destroyed. This narrative function, however, makes the statement about "these great buildings" far more prominent in the overall story (than if it is read merely as the introduction of "chapter 13"). Following upon the confrontation that began with Jesus' symbolic prophetic demonstration of God's judgment of the Temple, this is the concluding announcement that God's condemnation will be realized in its destruction.

By the time Mark's story reaches the trial of Jesus before the high priests and elders, the audience has already heard episodes of Jesus' demonstration symbolizing God's destruction of the Temple, his parable announcing that "the owner of the vineyard" will come and destroy the tenants, and his statement/prediction that "the great buildings" of Jerusalem would be destroyed. It is no surprise then that in his trial Jesus is accused of having said that he would "destroy this temple made with hands" (14:58). Certain aspects of Mark's account of the trial, however, seem somewhat unclear. The accusers' testimony is supposedly "false" (14:57). That could simply be one aspect of the prominent motif in the episode that "many gave false testimony against him, and their testimony did not agree" (14:56). Indeed, even about the "false" charge that he said he would destroy the Temple, "their testimony did not agree" (14:59), and the trial quickly moves on to the key question, "Are you the messiah?" his answer to which evokes the decisive charge of "blasphemy"! An intriguing possibility, on the other hand, is that the "falseness" of the testimony pertains (subtly) to its form. The clever Markan narrator may be portraying the high priests and elders as thick-headed, unacquainted with the form of prophetic pronouncements and uncomprehending of their ominous import. In their density they think that in saying something like "I will destroy the temple" he meant that he himself would do so. But if he had delivered such an utterance in prophecy, then he would have been speaking as the mouthpiece of God, in the same way that earlier Israelite prophets had done.[18]

The form of the accusation against Jesus both in the trial and when he is hanging on the cross is a double saying: "I will destroy this temple that is made with hands, and in three days I will build another, not made with hands" (14:58; cf. 15:29). The temple "not made with hands" was previously taken as a "spiritual" or "heavenly" temple. Since the discovery of the Dead Sea Scrolls, however, we have evidence of a Judean community contemporary to the Jesus movement that understood itself as the "temple." Since the Temple in Jerusalem had become hopelessly evil, the priestly-scribal Qumran community understood itself in terms of temple-ritual imagery (1QS 5:5-7; 8:4-10; 9:3-6; 4QFlor 1:1-13). Terms such as "house," "temple," "body," and "assembly" could all function as synonyms, usually with reference to a social body (the people). This enabled the Gospel of John, for example, to interpret Jesus' saying about destroying and rebuilding the Temple in terms of the resurrection of Jesus' body (John 2:12-22). In sections of *1 Enoch* the term "house" refers to the people, with "tower" being used for the Temple, which was polluted and was not expected to be rebuilt in the future restoration of the people. In Mark's story it seems that we should understand Jesus' prophecy about building "another [temple] not made with hands" similarly in the sense of the house or people of Israel. That would fit well with the rest of the Gospel in which Jesus is spearheading a renewal of Israel as a new Moses and Elijah, as we shall discuss in the next chapter. If the renewed people itself were understood as the true "temple" or "house" of God, then of course there would be no need for a temple-state, which was an imperial institution in the first place. The parallel to Q 13:28-29, 34-35 is striking. In Jesus' prophecy the destruction of the Temple is juxtaposed with the building or renewal of the people, now free of the oppressive ruling institutions.

This survey of the representation of Jesus in Q and Mark suggests some significant generalizations about the historical Jesus' opposition to the Temple and high priesthood. The Gospel story of Mark and the Q speeches are, of course, representations, and do not provide direct evidence, like a videotape or transcript, of Jesus' actions and speech-acts. That Jesus must have spoken, probably repeatedly, some prophetic statement against the Temple (as in Mark 14:58 and 5:29) is confirmed by the appearance of various versions in other Jesus literature such as *Gospel of Thomas* 71 and John 2:14-22. But the saying that stands isolated from any wider literary or historical meaning context in *Gospel of Thomas* 71 illustrates how the modern scholarly isolation and thus decontextualization of Jesus-sayings leads only to historical cul-de-sacs. And the way John's Gospel pointedly transforms a saying directed against the Temple, in the context of a violent demonstration against it, into a prophecy about Jesus' body illustrates that, like Mark, John knew this Jesus-tradition as a prophetic statement against the Temple. The appearance of these Jesus-sayings in *Thomas* and John simply further illustrates why we must focus on Mark and Q as the earliest Gospel sources that provide a literary context necessary to give at least some indication of the historical meaning context of Jesus' materials.

Mark and Q offer us the results of how Jesus' speech and action affected and took on significance for his followers in a particular historical situation as they referenced Israelite tradition. That is the fabric of historical events out of which historical significance emerges. Obviously, we should not imagine that Jesus marched up into Jerusalem, demonstrated in the Temple, and confronted one ruling group after another in exactly the way portrayed by Mark's story. But the combination of two very different Gospel sources representing Jesus as proclaiming and / or enacting prophetic condemnations of the Temple and high priests strongly suggests that Jesus condemned the Jerusalem rulers. As a prophet leading a movement of renewal of Israel, in the tradition of Israelite prophets who had repeatedly opposed oppressive rulers, and in a historical situation of increasing conflict between the people and their Jerusalem rulers, Jesus evidently both pronounced and symbolically acted out God's condemnation of the Temple and high priests.

JESUS' PROPHETIC CONDEMNATION
OF ROMAN IMPERIAL RULE

The impression prevails that Jesus did not condemn Roman rule. The traditional view is that Jesus was preaching a spiritual kingdom, while Caesar headed the temporal kingdom—but we now recognize that as a later self-protective and accommodationist Christian projection. We take another look, following our contextual-relational approach.

Tribute to Caesar

In one of the confrontations between Jesus and the Jerusalem rulers, the Pharisees and Herodians attempt to entrap Jesus with the question about whether the tribute to Rome is lawful. If we want to hear Jesus' response in its historical context of Israelite peoples under Roman imperial rule, then we must cut through the modern assumption about the separation of religion from political-economic affairs. The Pharisees and Herodians would presumably have known very well that it was *not* lawful, according to Mosaic covenantal law, to pay tribute to Rome. They also would have known that not to pay the tribute would have been taken by the Romans as tantamount to rebellion. Indeed, it would have been suicidal, since the Romans might well have again slaughtered and enslaved the people in vicious retaliation, as they had in 4 B.C.E. In fact, little more than two decades prior to Jesus' mission in Galilee and confrontation in Jerusalem, some of those Pharisees' predecessors had helped organize resistance to the tribute as leaders of the Fourth Philosophy.

In his response Jesus subtly avoids the trap in their search for an excuse to arrest him as a rebel. "Give to Caesar the things that are Caesar's, and to God the things that are God's." Jesus does not directly answer "It is not lawful" to the question about the tribute. But his declaration would have been understood in just that way by every Israelite listening, including the Pharisees. He takes the same stand as the earlier Fourth Philosophy. If God is the exclusive Lord and Master, if the people of Israel live under the exclusive kingship of God, then all things belong to God, the implications for Caesar being fairly obvious. Jesus is clearly and simply reasserting the Israelite principle that Caesar, or any other imperial ruler, has no claim on the Israelite people, since God is their actual king and master.[19]

Roman Imperialism Implicated in Jesus' Exorcisms

The series of episodes in which Jesus exorcises demons and the discussions of the significance of Jesus' exorcisms in the Gospels indicate that precisely in his practice of exorcisms God's kingdom is defeating Roman rule.[20] Discernment of this has been blocked primarily by our isolation of Gospel stories and sayings, but also by our inability to understand the phenomenon of demon possession in historical cultural context. That stories of Jesus' healings and exorcisms originally circulated as isolated individual stories is a modern scholarly projection. Two of the three exorcism stories in Mark's Gospel appear as components of sets of five stories, apparently in the sequence of sea crossing, exorcism, healing, healing, and wilderness feeding. The miracle stories in John's Gospel were apparently components of a similar series. To people rooted in Israelite tradition, such sets of stories clearly resonated with collective memories of Moses and Elijah, the leaders of Israel's exodus origins and its struggle against Ahab's oppressive kingship, respectively.

That is, Jesus' exorcisms, along with his healings and feedings, were key components in his role, not as an ordinary magician (a role in many traditional societies), but more particularly as a prophet like Moses and Elijah establishing a renewal of the people of Israel.

The exorcism stories and discussions of the significance of his exorcisms in the Beelzebul controversy stories, however, carry a distinctive dimension in the early Synoptic Gospel materials, discernible particularly in Mark but also in Q. First, in the initial exorcism in Mark, Jesus does not "cast out" (*ekballein*) the unclean spirit, but "vanquishes" (*epitiman*) it.[21] The latter meaning can be discerned from usage in texts such as Psalms (9:6; 68:30; 76:6; 80:16), Zechariah (3:2), and now in the Dead Sea Scrolls. In those passages, the term *epitiman* in Greek, translating *ga'ar* in Aramaic and Hebrew, was used with reference to Yahweh/God coming in judgment against foreign imperial regimes who had subjected Israel, or Yahweh subjecting Satan, or God vanquishing the spirits of Belial who were attempting to lead the people away from the covenant (1QM 14:9-11). That is, *ga'ar/epitiman* refers to the decisive action by which God or God's representative brings demonic powers into submission, and establishes the rule/kingdom of God and the deliverance of Israel. The "unclean spirit" (Mark 2:24) indicates precisely what is happening: "Have you come to destroy us?" Note the plural "us." The unclean spirit knows who Jesus is and what he is doing: Jesus is God's agent whose "kingdom of God" program of vanquishing demons is bringing defeat to all the demonic forces. But what do the demonic forces represent?

The next exorcism story in Mark (5:1-20), if we have ears to hear, brings another revelation about "what's happening" in the lives of the people in Galilee and round about. When the demon is exorcised, it is possible for it to be identified. Its name is Legion. The original hearers would have recognized immediately that "Legion" referred to Roman troops. For in their recent experience, Roman legions had burned the villages around such towns as Magdala and Sepphoris and slaughtered or enslaved thousands of their parents or grandparents. Moreover, in a series of military images, Legion is "dismissed" to enter the "troop" of swine, who then "charge" headlong down the slope as if into battle but are instead "drowned in the sea," suggesting not the lake but the Mediterranean Sea, whence they had originally come to conquer the people. Note that the imagery of "charging down into the sea" and being "drowned in the sea" would have immediately evoked memories of the destruction of Pharaoh's armies pursuing the Israelites but "drowned in the Reed Sea" as God liberated the people of Israel. As Jesus exorcised the alien forces that had possessed the people it was possible to recognize the identity of those alien occupying forces, that is, the Roman armies.[22] By implication, in Jesus' exorcisms those Roman soldiers, Legion, were being sent to their destruction in the sea.

Mark and Q have parallel discussions of the significance of Jesus' exorcisms in variant Beelzebul discourses (Mark 3:22-27; Q 11:14-20), which indicate that this was a very early understanding in the original Jesus movement. The Beelzebul discourses presuppose and are stated in terms that understand life's circumstances as involving a struggle between God and demonic forces headed by Satan. Modern interpreters simply assume that this is a religious understanding of the world, and that it is. But it is no less a political understanding. Note the political images in which the struggle is understood: both "house" and "kingdom," synonyms in fact, are terms for political rule,[23] and that is the point of the discussion. As in the Dead Sea Scrolls, God's kingdom is involved in a struggle for domination of human life, of history, with the opposing demonic forces of Satan. This was one of the principal ways that Galilean peasants as well as Qumran scribes had of explaining how they could be suffering such subjection and even violent oppression, when supposedly God was the ruler of history. Opposing forces of overwhelming superhuman strength must be responsible.

This was a self-protective explanation and mode of understanding of the forces that had subjugated them. It kept them from launching a suicidal revolt that would likely have evoked Roman retaliation. But it was also a mystifying explanation, for it veiled the real, concrete forces that were oppressing them, the imperial Roman conquests, governors, and troops. While similar to the severe dualism of Light versus Darkness, God versus Belial, at Qumran, the more popular demonology also exhibits some significant differences. The popular belief in demon possession is more ad hoc, less systematic than the scribal view articulated in the Community Rule and War Scroll from Qumran. The Qumranites believed that they were already living under the Spirit of Light, but that history was still under the sway of the Prince of Belial for the foreseeable future, until God should finally take action to end that domination. The popular Galilean way of handling their subjugation to foreign forces took the form of individual demon possession, as well as belief in their general subjugation to alien forces.

In the context of that belief, the Beelzebul discourses, like the exorcism stories just examined, declare that precisely in Jesus' exorcisms God is accomplishing a political as well as a religious or spiritual victory. Jesus is not merely a magician with special powers. Rather, in the exorcisms, in which Satan's goods are being plundered (i.e., his demons exorcised), Satan's rule or kingdom is being overcome. This is stated implicitly in Mark 3:27 and explicitly in Q 11:20, in another vivid allusion to God's victory over the Egyptian magicians in the exodus story. "If, by 'the finger of God' I cast out demons, then the kingdom of God has come upon you."

In Jesus' exorcisms, however, the demons were identified as Roman legions, just as at Qumran the Romans armies were understood to be the human political forces under the power of the Prince of Darkness. By implication, therefore, God's victory over Satan manifested in Jesus' exorcisms meant that Roman rule was being overcome as well. Jesus' followers were under no illusion that the Roman armies had suddenly disappeared from Palestine. But they understood and declared that the ultimate significance of Jesus' exorcisms was the defeat of Roman rule.

Woven throughout these passages in which Jesus as prophet pronounces God's condemnation of oppressive rulers and oppressive institutional structures appears the theme that seems to holds them all together. Implicit and virtually explicit in the Markan exorcism stories and Beelzebul discourse, and explicit in the Q Beelzebul discourse, the exorcisms are manifestations of the kingdom of God being established over and among the people even as it defeats and terminates the domination of Satan and the Romans. Jesus' statement about rendering to Caesar and to God presupposes and implicitly reasserts the sole rule or kingdom of God, again over against that of the Roman imperialism. Presupposed and implicit in all of the prophetic pronouncements and oracles against the Temple and high-priestly rulers is that God is the ultimate ruler who judges exploitative rulers and institutions.

The judgmental side of the kingdom of God in Mark's and Q's representation of Jesus, however, is not particularly vengeful. The prophetic double saying(s) that God (Jesus) would destroy the Jerusalem Temple and build another temple or house, not made with human hands, suggests that God's destructive rule has a constructive counterpart in building or renewing the people as God's real house or temple. Indeed, the evidently linked prophetic sayings in Q 13:28-29 and 34-35 suggest that the imminent desolation of the ruling house of Jerusalem was the counterpart of the imminent banquet of the kingdom of God. That is, not only is the kingdom of God the overarching theme of Jesus' prophetic declaration of judgment against Roman rulers and their clients in Jerusalem, but that judgmental face of the kingdom had a constructive counterpart of deliverance, empowerment, and renewal for the people. In modern political discourse, in the judgmental side of the kingdom of God, Jesus was proclaiming that God was in the process of effecting the "political revolution" that would overthrow the Roman imperial order in Palestine. Then, on the constructive side, in the confidence that God was taking care of the dominant political order, Jesus and his movement were carrying out the "social revolution" that God was making possible and empowering in Galilean village communities. That is social revolution, the subject of the next chapter.

In this survey of the judgmental aspect of the kingdom of God, we have explored how (1) in the crisis of social disintegration under Roman conquest and imperial rule through the Judean priestly aristocracy, and (2) drawing heavily on the Israelite tradition of rejection of oppressive rulers under the exclusive kingship of God, (3) Jesus assumed (4) the traditional role of prophetic spokesperson for God and leader of the people in (5) pronouncing and demonstrating God's condemnation of intolerable rulers so that renewal of the society was possible. In all of these respects Jesus was thoroughly embedded in and understandable in terms of the historical context of the Israelite people under Roman imperial rule.

Roman conquest and imposition of client rulers, with the resulting multiple layers of taxes and socially disintegrative economic and cultural practices, set the conditions of and for Jesus' mission and other, parallel movements (as surveyed in chapter 1). In generating and articulating his program, moreover, Jesus drew thoroughly on Israelite traditions of opposition to imperial and oppressive domestic rulers. There is no need to debate whether he was "apocalyptic," because both Jesus and the apocalypses produced by scribal groups shared the widespread common Israelite pattern of God's judgment against foreign rulers as a prerequisite of restoration of the subject people, a pattern dictated by the recurrent circumstances of Israelite peoples under imperial rule. In this regard Jesus stands together with activist Pharisees and other teachers and administrators who formed resistance groups such as the Fourth Philosophy. They stand on precisely the same grounds in rejecting the tribute to Rome: they owe exclusive loyalty to God as their only ruler and lord. Surely the vast majority of Judeans and Galileans believed that, and attempted to resist Roman exploitation in whatever ways they could whenever they could (all explored in chapter 2).

In catalyzing a movement and carrying out his "kingdom of God" program, Jesus adapted traditional social roles that remained alive in his society, as we know because some of his contemporaries stepped into the same roles. In pronouncing God's judgment on the Temple he became a latter-day Jeremiah, even reciting a prophecy of his famous precursor. Continuation of oracular prophecy against Jerusalem rule was very much alive in the first century, as we know from the other Jesus, son of Hananiah, who also pronounced a prophetic lament against the ruling city. Beyond the scope of Jesus ben Hananiah and other oracular prophets, however, Jesus ben Joseph was leader of a popular movement opposed to the Jerusalem power brokers who served as clients for the higher imperial rule of Rome. In this regard Jesus also shared a role with another prophet who led a popular movement, the Egyptian-Jewish prophet who led his followers to the Mount of Olives, where they were to witness the collapse of the city walls (apparently Jericho-style) and the disappearance of Roman rule. It is surely in the role of a prophet leading a popular movement that Jesus, like his paradigmatic predecessors Moses and Elijah, performed healings and exorcisms that manifested the victory of God's rule over that of the Romans. In all of these respects, Jesus of Nazareth belongs in the same context with and stands shoulder to shoulder with these other leaders of movements among the Judean and Galilean people, and pursues the same general agenda in parallel paths: independence from Roman imperial rule so that the people can again be empowered to renew their traditional way of life under the rule of God.

COVENANTAL COMMUNITY AND COOPERATION

> *The vast majority of people have been and continue to be not citizens but subjects. So long as we confine our conception of the political to activity that is openly declared we are driven to conclude that subordinate groups essentially lack a political life or that what political life they do have is restricted to those exceptional moments of popular explosion. To do so is to miss the immense political terrain that lies between quiescence and revolt and that, for better or worse, is the political environment of subject classes.*
>
> —James C. Scott

In the confidence that the Roman imperial order stood under the judgment of God's imminent kingdom, Jesus launched a mission of social renewal among subject peoples. In contrast to some of the scribal intellectuals who were waiting patiently for God's decisive "intervention in history" to terminate imperial rule, Jesus and his followers understood God to be acting already in the people's lives and communities. The imperial order was still in place. Convinced that Roman rulers and their Herodian and high-priestly clients had been condemned by God, however, Jesus acted to heal the effects of empire and to summon people to rebuild their community life. In the conviction that the kingdom of God was at hand, he pressed a program of social revolution to reestablish just egalitarian and mutually supportive social-economic relations in the village communities that constituted the basic form of the people's life.

HEALING THE EFFECTS OF IMPERIALISM

Roman military power may have established a "new world order" of "peace and security" for the imperial elite, and its extraction of goods from the provinces may have provided "bread and circus" for the people of the imperial metropolis. The ugly underside of the Pax Romana, however, was disorder and devastation for subject peoples. Partly because they resisted the new imperial order, Galileans and Judeans suffered slaughter, enslavement, and destruction of their homes and villages (chapter 1). The escalating economic demands resulting from multiple layers of rulers in Palestine compounded the imperial impact on the social order. Gospel literature portrays a people that is heavily indebted and hungry, plagued by physical and social paralysis, and generally despairing about its circumstances. In some cases alien demonic forces ("unclean spirits") had taken control, driving people into self-destructive behavior. Even the fundamental social forms of family and village community were disintegrating under the pressures of the Roman imperial order.

The standard approach pictures Jesus as dealing primarily with individuals, both in his teachings and in his healings and exorcisms. According to the Christian theological scheme that underlies this approach, Jesus did not found a movement or community. Only later, after the resurrection appearances, did his "followers" form a community, in Jerusalem, far from the scene of his ministry in Galilee. A particularly intriguing version of this depoliticized individualistic approach pictures Jesus as having taught individuals to abandon their homes and families for a radical lifestyle of itinerant beggars, a "hippie" life somewhat like that of the ancient Cynic philosophers.[1] This Jesus advocated the violation of time-honored social customs that held families and communities together, that is, the Israelite covenantal tradition that guided social interaction. The effect of such an individualistic enterprise, of course, would have been to exacerbate the social disintegration in Palestinian peasant society that Roman imperialism had already generated. Urging people to abandon their families' ancestral lands and to beg food from villagers who were having trouble feeding their own families would only have further undermined the family and village communities that constituted the fundamental social forms of life in ancient Syria-Palestine.

In striking contrast with this individualistic modern projection, however, the Gospels usually portray Jesus dealing with people in social contexts and relations. He speaks and performs healings and exorcisms in the context of village assemblies or ad hoc gatherings, often with relatives or friends bringing the person to be healed or summoning the healer. His dialogues in "pronouncement stories," many of which are debates with the Pharisees, address issues of social and economic relations. Jesus' speeches not only address groups of people but deal with social relations in social context. Even in the particular sayings that comprise Jesus' speeches we can discern the *context* addressed from the *content* of the sayings.[2] If, as part of our relational-contextual approach, we can cut through modern individualism and attend to the social relations indicated in our earliest Gospel sources, we see Jesus as healing, not exacerbating, the effects of imperialism among Galilean and nearby people in four interrelated ways.

Expelling Alien Occupying Forces

The portrayal of Jesus' exorcisms in Mark and Q indicates that at all levels Jesus was exposing and expelling, even defeating, the demonic forces (which, once exposed, were associated with Roman imperialism) at three interrelated levels, as discussed in chapter 4. At the most fundamental, phenomenological level, the effects of possession by such alien forces were violent antisocial and self-destructive behavior (Mark 5:2-5; 9:18). Jesus commands power/authority over these "unclean spirits" (1:22, 27). He not only expels them but "defeats" them (1:23-26). Thus liberated from the "occupying" alien force, the person returns to a rightful state of mind and social life (5:15, 20).

Possession by "unclean spirits" was part of the more general social-spiritual condition of being constantly under attack or even control by a superhuman destructive force, Satan, the "prince of demons," who was engaged in a sustained struggle with God for control of society and history. This explanation of their situation enabled Galileans and Judeans to avoid blaming themselves. This (partially) self-protective representation of their situation kept them from taking suicidal action against the overwhelming forces that effectively controlled their lives.

The dialogues about Beelzebul in both Mark (3:22-28) and Q (11:14-20) assert that at this overarching spiritual level Jesus' exorcisms indicated that God was finally winning the struggle against Satan.

At the political level, finally, Satan/Belial and the demons were working though or were represented by the Romans, as in the War Scroll from Qumran. At the more popular level of Mark's Gospel, it becomes clear once Jesus drives out the demon (whose name is "Legion") that it is really the Romans who are "possessing" the people—and by implication Jesus' exorcisms are freeing the people from Roman oppression.

Healing the Social Body

Like the exorcisms, Jesus' healings were not simply isolated acts of individual mercy, but part of a larger program of social as well as personal healing. The healing episodes in Mark's story that appear in sequences with sea crossings and wilderness feedings evoke memories of Moses and Elijah, the great founding and renewing prophets of Israel. In these healings and other "miracles," therefore, Mark's story represents Jesus as engaged in a renewal of Israel—or of Israel plus other peoples, in that some of the incidents involve people in the villages beyond the frontiers of Galilee.

On the now widely accepted assumption that Jesus did indeed perform healings of various kinds, we must imagine dozens of individual healings and healing stories. Stories of particular healings were retold as, and because, they resonated with hearers.[3] The stories that survived the winnowing process of repeated oral performances would have been the ones that resonated most widely with multiple audiences, that is, the ones that "spoke to" the general malaise of the people who heard them. Thus not only was the original healing (to which we have no direct access) both a healing of a particular person and embedded in social relationships, but each healing story was both a healing of a particular person and a continuing "healing" of the social "body" of subsequent communities of hearers.

Not surprisingly, then, the individual people healed in the typical stories that are selected for inclusion in the more comprehensive Gospel stories such as Mark's are also representative figures. This is particularly evident in the healing episodes in the series of stories in which Jesus is enacting a renewal of Israel, most dramatically perhaps in the healings of the two women in Mark 5:21-43. Both the woman who had been hemorrhaging for *twelve* years and the nearly dead *twelve*-year-old girl clearly represent the people of Israel, which consisted symbolically of twelve tribes. The original hearers of the Gospel would have known tacitly and implicitly—and we can reconstruct by historical investigation—that both the individual and the social hemorrhaging and near death were the effects of the people's subjection to imperial forces. Thus as the woman's faith that special powers are working through Jesus, leading her to take the initiative in touching his garment, results in her healing, so also the people's trust that God's restorative powers are working through Jesus is leading to their recovery from the death-dealing domination by Roman imperial rule. When Jesus brings the seemingly dead twelve-year-old girl back to life just at the time she has come of age to produce children, he is mediating new life to Israel in general. In these and other episodes Jesus is healing the illnesses brought on by Roman imperialism.

Instilling Hope in a Hopeless Situation

The content of several speeches in Q and punch lines of episodes in Mark indicate that Jesus was offering and instilling hope in the seemingly hopeless situation of a people languishing under foreign domination and its effects. To people in despair over their poverty and hunger, Jesus declares, "Blessed are you who mourn, for you shall rejoice" (Q 6:20-22). In reply to John's disciples' question whether he is the promised "coming one," Jesus points to the fulfillment of age-old Israelite longings that the blind would see, the lame walk, and the poor have good news preached to them (Q 7:18-23). The recent appearance of John, who had preached justice and boldly criticized Herod Antipas, must have offered hope; Jesus declares that the kingdom he has offered them is so astoundingly wonderful that "even the least in the kingdom of God will be greater than John" (Q 7:24-28). To people who are anxious about where the next meal will come from and how they can clothe themselves Jesus declares that subsistence needs will take care of themselves (in mutual sharing?) if they single-mindedly pursue the kingdom (Q 12:22-31).

Galileans and others of Israelite heritage explained their suffering as punishment for their own or their parents' sins in violation of the covenant commandments. As Jesus heals his paralysis, he declares to the man lowered into the house by his friends, "son, your sins are forgiven" (Mark 2:1-9)—thus freeing up the life energies that had previously been introjected in self-blame and dysfunctional paralysis. By evoking cultural memories of God's great acts of deliverance in the history of Israel's origins, such as the sea crossings and wilderness feedings, the episodes of Jesus' sea crossings with the twelve disciples (representatives of Israel) and his feedings of thousands in the wilderness would evoke hope among the hearers that a new exodus is under way in Jesus' mission and movement. Many of the parables in Mark 4 and Q constitute reassuring analogies that would evoke confidence among the hearers about how, despite inauspicious appearances, the kingdom of God is growing effectively so that it will result in an astounding "harvest" or "bumper crop" never before experienced by peasant farmers.

Counteracting Social Disintegration

Far from calling people to leave their families and to abandon social customs and norms, thus exacerbating the social disintegration already under way in Syria-Palestine, Jesus attempted to reinforce family and social solidarity.

In response to an accusation by the scribes and Pharisees, Jesus accused them of inducing peasants to support the Temple through the device of "Corban," that is, "devotion" of goods (produce of a field?), which meant they could no longer be used to support one's elderly parents (Mark 7:1-13). Appealing to the basic covenantal "commandment of God"—"Honor your father and mother" is the pointed example—as the sole basis of social relations, Jesus insisted that local use of peasant resources must take priority over support of the Temple. When the Pharisees tested him on the issue of divorce, he threw their (Jerusalem's "great tradition") version of the Law of Moses back in their face as having been given to them "for their hardness of heart." It is likely that their "liberal" divorce laws (based on Deut 24:1-4) were useful for well-to-do families in consolidating their landholding through the device of divorce and remarriage. Such maneuvering was also taking advantage of deeply indebted families, one more factor exacerbating the disintegration of marriage and family units. By forbidding divorce and remarriage, in appeal to the creation stories of the solidarity of husband and wife, Jesus was reinforcing the marriage bond as the essential core of the fundamental social form of the family.

Besides attempting to reinforce the family as a social unit, Jesus apparently also encouraged village communities to take up the slack in light of the disintegration of some family units. This appears to be the message of a passage that, ironically, has been taken as Jesus' rejection of his own family (Mark 3:31-35). This passage is the concluding episode in Jesus' campaign of renewal in Galilean villages, an intermediate conclusion of the story so far. The mother and brothers standing outside merely provide the foil for the punch line of the episode: "Whoever does the will of God is my brother and sister and mother." Jesus does not reject his family here. He rather calls the villagers gathered in this house to form a "familial" community in doing the will of God. What he means by "the will of God" is perhaps most evident in Matthew's version of the Lord's Prayer, where it parallels "the kingdom of God." In Israelite tradition "the will of God" was known in and functioned as a synonym for the Mosaic covenant. Indeed, as evident in key speeches and dialogues in Q and Mark, renewal of the Mosaic covenant formed the very core of Jesus' renewal of the people in their village communities.

WORKING IN VILLAGE COMMUNITIES

Mark portrays Jesus' mission as focused on village communities, the fundamental social form in which the people's life is embodied in any peasant society. In the first step of the story Jesus' campaign in the villages of Galilee has its "headquarters" in the village of Capernaum, at the north shore of the Sea of Galilee, opposite the new capital city of Tiberias (1:21; 2:1; 6:6).[4] From this base he had easy access to other villages in the area. Similarly, when he moves beyond Galilee into other "regions" he works, for example, "in the villages of Caesarea Philippi." When Jesus repeatedly goes into a/their "synagogue," he is not going into a religious building, but into a local village assembly (1:21; 3:1; 6:1). Something that is simply assumed in Mark's narrative and by its hearers, but that we can reconstruct by extrapolation from later rabbinic sources, is that these assemblies met once or twice a week. So Jesus was deliberately visiting a given village on days that the people would be assembled for community discussion, business, and prayers. In that context he carried out his teaching and healing and exorcism. He was pointedly dealing with whole communities, not just individuals, in the context of their meeting for self-governance. He was not dealing only with what we moderns call "religious" matters, but with the more general political-economic concerns of the village communities as well, as we shall see below.

The most telling indications that Jesus' mission of proclamation and manifestation of the kingdom of God focused on village communities are the "mission discourses" in Mark (6:7-13) and Q (9:57—10:16). The strikingly parallel structure of the two mission discourses from two different branches of the Jesus movement provides a clear indication that the basic unit of communication was (at least) the whole discourse, not separate sayings. The parallel structure includes, in sequence, a statement of sending, instructions on what to take or not to take for the journey, and instructions for staying in households and on how the envoys are to respond to towns/places that welcome them and those that reject them. What was apparently part of the instructions for healing and preaching in the receptive towns in Q appears in Mark's narrative framing at the close of the speech.

The likelihood that the Q mission speech was introduced by the set of parallel sayings in Q 9:57-62 also means that it referenced the popular Israelite tradition of Elijah's commissioning of Elisha.[5] The phrases "leaving the dead to bury the dead" and "putting one's hand to the plow and not looking back" clearly allude to stories of Elijah's call of Elisha to continue his mission for the renewal of Israel in resistance to Ahab's oppressive rule.[6] We might discern a similar feature in the larger narrative context of Jesus' mission speech in Mark. Mark gives multiple signals that Jesus is a new Elijah, including his healings and his appearance on the mountain with Elijah as well as Moses. In a further connection with the mission speech, therefore, it is noteworthy that immediately after his baptism by John, Jesus, like Elijah, spends forty days in the wilderness being tested as a prophet, whereupon his first action is to call disciples, as Elijah did Elisha, to help in the renewal of Israel. The mission discourses are therefore unmistakably presented as an important step in Jesus' general mission of renewal of Israel.

In this meaning context, then, it is highly significant that both the Markan and the Q mission speeches include several indications that the mission focused on villages, not just on individuals or households. Households, in fact, cannot be separated from the villages of which they were component members. First, physically, insofar as the rooms of each household were directly connected with those of other households in a dense settlement, a couple of visitors would be obvious to the whole village. They would unavoidably have interacted with more than the household in which they were staying. Second, in both the Mark and Q discourses it is their reception or rejection by the village (place or town) that determines how the envoys respond: with the peace and healing of the kingdom of God for any and all in the village or by calling down divine judgment on the whole village. This further indicates that villages as whole communities were the focus of their mission. Finally, the envoys are to remain in the villages, based in one household, for a period of time. One detects a certain strategy of mission here. Along with their proclaiming the kingdom and performing healings and exorcisms, the envoys appear to be engaged in community organizing, helping the village to get its act together.

We cannot avoid the conclusion that, as portrayed in both the Markan and the Q mission discourses, the very context and focus of Jesus' mission of preaching and healing was the local village community. It would have been impossible for Jesus to have worked in Galilee without dealing with the basic social form in which the people lived their lives. As we shall see below, many of his speeches in Q and teachings in Mark involve village communities as the context and local interaction as their subject. No wonder Jesus is not represented as "founding" a new community. Communities already existed. Everyone Jesus dealt with was embedded in a community. Those communities, however, were struggling, and Jesus' mission was addressed precisely to them.

RENEWING COVENANTAL COMMUNITIES

Renewal of the Mosaic covenant is a major theme in both the Gospel of Mark and the speeches in Q. In Christian theological interpretation, the revelation Jesus brought was a decisive move beyond the Mosaic covenantal law to the gospel of salvation that believers would appropriate by faith. Interpreters of the Hebrew Bible (Old Testament), however, have long since recognized that, in theological terms, the Mosaic covenant includes gospel along with law. Indeed, the very form of the Mosaic covenant begins with the declaration of God's deliverance in the exodus from Egyptian bondage as the basis of the people's obligation to observe the covenant law.

The Mosaic covenant was, in effect, a "constitution," a constituting set of principles, for early Israel as an independent agrarian people. Economic and political relations were integral to the covenant and utterly inseparable from the religious dimension. In contrast with other peasantries, according to the Mosaic covenant, Israel had no human king or other overlord taking a portion of their produce, because God was their king, their exclusive overlord. The first four of the Ten Commandments articulated and protected the people's exclusive loyalty to their God. The next six commandments focused on social-economic relations in the two fundamental forms of peasant society, the family and relations among (heads of) families in village communities. The Mosaic covenant thus provided the fundamental framework and principles for community life in the villages of Israel. If we attend to the social function of those "commandments" it is clear that the emphasis lay on economic relations. The last six commandments, along with the closely related mechanisms of the wider covenantal tradition in the Hebrew Bible, thus functioned to keep people from gaining power over one another and to keep each family economically viable in its community. Of course, economic viability has been the central concern of most people in most of history, since the vast majority of people who have ever lived were peasants. The Mosaic covenant comprised ancient Israel's articulation of what has been called the "moral economy" of peasant societies.[7]

The Davidic monarchy established tributary political-economic relations legitimated religiously by service of God in the Temple. Yet despite and pointedly over against their economic exploitation by monarchy and Temple, Israelite villagers continued to carry on local social-economic life according to covenantal principles that guarded the fundamental social-economic rights of family units. Prophets such as Amos, Micah, and Jeremiah applied these principles also to relations between the monarchy and the peasantry. Micah (2:1-5) appealed directly to the covenantal commandments in his indictment of the powerful: "They covet fields, and seize them; houses, and take them away; they oppress . . . people and their inheritance." Jeremiah (7:1-15) went so far as to declare that the whole institution of the Temple and its high priests would be destroyed by Yahweh because they systematically violated the covenantal commandments prohibiting exploitation. These repeated applications of covenantal principles even to kings, royal officers, and Temple officials by the prophets, many of whom were rooted in village life, suggest that the Israelite villagers held each other accountable to the commandments.

There are a number of indications that the Mosaic covenant was deeply rooted and still operational in Judean and Galilean society at the time of Jesus. That the scholar-teacher Hillel devised the famous *prosbul* that supposedly eased credit by enabling creditors to avoid the sabbatical cancellation of debts means that the principle was still viewed as valid (Mishnah *Shebi'it* 10:3-7; cf. Deut 15:1-6).[8] The whole society evidently continued to observe the sabbatical rest of the land, judging from Josephus's reports on how it figured in famines and the Roman levy of tribute (Exod 23:10-11; *Ant.* 3.280–81; 12.378; 13.235; 14.202, 206, 475; 15.7). Even more pertinent to Jesus and his program is the prominence of the covenant in the Dead Sea Scrolls. The Community Rule in particular illustrates how even a scribal-priestly group could use the Mosaic covenant as the basis for declaring their independence of the incumbent high-priestly rulers in Jerusalem and establishing an independent, relatively egalitarian community life featuring mutual sharing and strict observance of covenantal principles.

If we listen with ears attuned to Israelite tradition, we hear the covenantal theme at prominent points in Mark and Q. In the Q speech where Jesus teaches the prayer for the kingdom (the Lord's Prayer, 11:2-4, 9-13), we hear a series of petitions about concrete economic matters such as subsistence bread. Another of those petitions is "cancel our debts, as we herewith forgive those of our debtors." That petition clearly alludes to one of the principal Mosaic covenantal devices by which Israelite society attempted to keep family units viable in their village communities. Debts were to be canceled every seven years—and debt slaves released, and so on (Deut 15:1-6; Exod 21:1-7; Leviticus 25), key mechanisms in the moral economy of the Israelite peasantry. Significantly, Matthew's community clearly understood the opening petition of the prayer ("Your kingdom come!") in covenantal terms, as indicated by the parallel phrase, "Your will be done (on earth as in heaven)." Doing the will of God meant observing the covenantal commandments.

In Mark's story, as the confrontation between Jesus and the high-priestly rulers comes to a climax in Jerusalem precisely at the Passover celebration of the exodus liberation from foreign rule, Jesus celebrates his "last supper" (Mark 14:17-25). We may already suspect that a meal with *the Twelve* has something to do with the renewal of Israel. Jesus declares, as he offers them the cup, "this is my blood of the covenant which is poured out for many." This is clearly a gesture parallel to the ritual that solemnized the Mosaic covenant when given originally on Sinai. Jesus' words over the cup refer to Moses throwing one basin of blood over the people and another over the altar (representing God), thus binding (in one blood or life) the parties to the covenant. Jesus' renewal of the Mosaic covenant at the Last Supper should alert us to other re-assertions of the covenant in Mark's story, such as his insistence on the basic "commandment of God" in contrast to the Pharisees' "traditions of the elders" (Mark 7:1-13).

These other occurrences of Mosaic covenantal themes in Mark and Q serve to prepare us to recognize that both the longest speech in Q (6:20-49) and the series of dialogues in Mark with which Jesus' mission in the villages of Palestine concludes (Mark 10:2-45) are renewals of Mosaic covenant. The exorcisms, healings, forgiveness, and procla-mation of the kingdom's presence/immanence empowered the people by overcoming the symptoms of disintegration resulting from Roman imperialism. The key to the renewal of the people, however, was their social-economic relations in the village communities that constituted the basic framework of the people's common life. Tapping the people's reservoir of cultural tradition, Jesus pressed a renewal of Mosaic cove-nant to foster and guide a renewal of cooperative *covenantal* community.

Jesus' Covenant Renewal Speech in Q

Both in the long speech in Q 6:20-49 and in the series of dialogues in Mark 10:2-45 Jesus makes several clear references to traditional covenantal teachings. In the Markan dialogues he even explicitly recites the covenant commandments. Most striking of all (once we become at-tentive to broader patterns in the cultural tradition), the Q speech ref-erences basic structural components of the Mosaic covenant. The presence of these component elements of the Mosaic covenant that was so central to Israelite social life and cultural tradition suggests that we should investigate further the broader covenantal pattern that underlies and informs these speeches.

As we learn in Hebrew Bible (Old Testament) introductory courses, the basic structure of the Mosaic covenant consisted of three major components:

1. a statement of God's deliverance that evokes the gratitude and obligation of the delivered (to keep the ensuing principles);
2. principles of exclusive loyalty to God and principles of societal relations;
3. sanctions, such as witnesses and blessings and curses, as motivation for observance.[9]

From the original giving of the covenant on Sinai in Exodus 20, the covenant renewal ceremony in Joshua 24, and the elaborated covenant and covenantal teaching in book of Deuteronomy, it appears that the earliest covenant focused on

1. God's deliverance from Egyptian bondage in the exodus;
2. the Ten Commandments; and
3. blessings and curses in future life as a result of keeping or not keeping the commandments.

The Community Rule from Qumran now gives us evidence from outside of Jesus traditions that the Mosaic covenant in its basic structure was alive and well in Roman-dominated Palestine. In the covenant renewal ceremony at Qumran, moreover, the blessings and curses were transformed into part of the statement of deliverance, now in the present and future rather than in previous history.[10] This continuation yet transformation of the covenant's structural components at Qumran enables us to see the parallel presence and transformation of covenant structure in Jesus' opening speech in Q 6:20-49 (a structure retained in the Sermon on the Mount in Matthew 5–7):[11]

1. The blessings and woes have been transformed into new statements of deliverance in the present and/or imminent future, with which Jesus' renewed covenant begins. (6:20-22)
2. The ensuing teachings not only allude to traditional covenantal teaching, but constitute renewed covenantal principles, consisting of (what have been called) "focal instances." (esp. 6:27-36)
3. Although the blessings and curses have been transformed into statements of new deliverance at the beginning of the speech, the third component, sanctions, is present, consisting of the double parable of building houses respectively on rock and sand, with which the speech closes. (6:43-49)

Besides taking the form of a renewed covenant, Jesus' opening speech in Q would have been regularly performed before a group of people with whom it resonated on the basis of their revered cultural tradition. It was "performative speech," speech that made something happen, like the minister in a wedding saying, "I now pronounce you husband and wife," or the judge in court saying, "Case dismissed." This speech, repeatedly performed in a group of people, probably in villages, was the charter for the communities of a movement, the charter of a society undergoing renewal.

Not only that, this covenantal renewal speech addressed the symptoms of the disintegration of the people's communities under the pressures of Roman imperialism and exploitation by the local Roman client rulers, as summarized above. The speech does this in the bold declarations of new deliverance that open the covenant renewal: "Blessed are the poor, for yours is the kingdom of God," and so on (Q 6:20-26). There are indications elsewhere in Jesus traditions that the people, precisely because they were rooted in covenant tradition, may have been blaming themselves. Insofar as they were suffering hunger, disease, and poverty, it was because they had sinned, by breaking the covenant laws. They were therefore now receiving the curses. This is surely what Jesus was addressing in his forgiveness of sins in connection with healings (as in Mark 2:1-12). In addressing the people's self-blame and despair, therefore, Jesus transforms the blessings and curses into a new declaration of God's assurance of deliverance for the poor and hungry and condemnation of those who were wealthy, almost certainly because they were expropriating the goods of the peasantry.

Having assured them of God's deliverance-in-process, in the next step of the covenant renewal, Jesus summons people to overcome their debilitating internal economic and social conflicts (Q 6:27-42).

First, in local *economic* relations, they must return to the time-honored values and principles of mutual sharing and cooperation central to covenantal teaching. Given increased economic pressures from their rulers, villagers would have been increasingly indebted to one another. Those who had borrowed would have been unable to repay the loans. Those who had previously aided their neighbors would have become desperate themselves, pressuring their debtor neighbors for repayment, resulting in increasing local conflict. Jesus addresses conflicts rooted in such economic pressures with the principle "Love your enemies." From the context indicated in the content of the ensuing focal instances we can see that local conflicts are addressed, not relations with Roman soldiers, who would not have been on the scene as an occupying army in any case.

Jesus briefly addresses debtors in the community (6:29). "If someone sues you for your cloak, let him take your shirt as well"—which of course means you would be standing stark naked, embarrassing your creditor in front of the whole village (Jesus has a sense of humor!). The reference is to the age-old covenant law code: "You shall not deal with others as a creditor. If you take your neighbor's cloak in pawn, you shall restore it before the sun goes down, since it is your neighbor's only covering at night" (Exod 22:25-27; Deut 24:10-13).

Jesus addresses mainly people in the community in their actual or perpetual role of aiding needy neighbors, insisting that they continue their sharing and generosity (Q 6:30-36). "To the one who asks from you give, and from the one who borrows do not ask back. . . . But love your enemies, and do good and lend." This is a broad general statement of social-economic cooperation and sharing reminiscent of any number of traditional covenantal teachings, as evident in the biblical covenant codes (e.g., Deut 15:7-11; cf. Sir 29:1). "Be merciful as your Father is merciful" patterns generosity within the community on the divine generosity, again resonating with age-old covenantal tradition, as evident in a similar principle enunciated in Leviticus 19:2. The admonitions and parallel rhetorical questions beginning with "Love your enemies" (Q 6:27-36) stand directly in the Mosaic covenantal tradition, build on it, and renew it. The focal instances of lending and borrowing here would have recalled the whole range of such traditional covenantal teachings to the minds of the listeners. The principles implicit in these focal instances bear a remarkable resemblance to the third petition in the Lord's Prayer: "Your kingdom come. . . . Cancel our debts, as we herewith forgive those of our debtors."

After focusing on local economic conflicts, Jesus addresses conflicts in local *social* interaction, probably conflicts that would have been related to the economic difficulties (6:37-42). "Do not judge and you will not be judged." Such admonitions are again deeply rooted in the tradition of Mosaic covenantal teaching, as evident through the window provided by Lev 19:17-18. Thus, after declaring the blessings of the imminent kingdom of God that give the people new hope, Jesus restates the fundamental covenantal principles of mutual sharing and cooperation in terms that would resonate deeply with the people.

The final section of the covenant renewal speech (Q 6:43-49), probing the motivational roots of covenantal behavior, also draws on already well-established covenantal tradition. Best known is surely the prophecy in Jer 31:27-34 of the new covenant written on the heart rather than on stone tablets, whereby people would spontaneously maintain covenantal justice in their social relations. The listing of the inner qualities or dispositions that result in certain behavior in the renewed covenant at Qumran (see 1QS 4:2-7, 9-12) provides yet another parallel. The double parable of houses built respectively on rock and sand (Q 6:46-49) provides the clinching sanction on the whole series of covenantal admonitions.

In summary, in his first and longest speech in Q, Jesus as a prophet like Moses enacts—in performative speech—the renewal of the covenant among groups of hearers. In that act the hearers are thus reconstituted as a covenanted community. The renewal of covenant addresses people whose village communities are disintegrating into economic and social conflicts between hard-pressed families over increasingly scarce resources for subsistence because of outside pressures or Roman imperialism and rigorous taxation by Roman client rulers. Indeed, such conflicts are dissolving the fabric of covenantal mutual sharing and cooperation that had traditionally held village communities together. The contents of the covenant renewal address these debilitating conflicts directly. After declaring the blessings of the imminent kingdom of God that give the people new hope, Jesus restates the fundamental covenantal principles of mutual sharing and cooperation in terms that would have resonated deeply with the people.

This is not just teaching, however, since it comes in the context of a reenactment of the covenant in which the people are making a recommitment to God and to one another as a community of solidarity and mutual caring. This involves more than merely respecting each other's economic rights by not coveting and stealing. Drawing on other principles of the covenantal tradition, Jesus here has the people recommit themselves to active sharing of scarce resources in a time when all are struggling. As in the prayer for the kingdom later in the sequence of Q speeches, the people commit themselves not only to extend loans to one another, but to cancel the debts of their debtors. This proactive covenantal commitment to community solidarity and sharing thus also serves as a strategy of resistance to the rulers, whose escalating aggrandizement depends on the further disintegration of those village communities so that, without the protection of mutual aid, peasants could be turned into sharecroppers economically dependent on their rulers.

Jesus' Covenant Renewal in Mark

The prominence of the covenant theme in Mark's overall story enables us to see how the series of dialogues at the close of Jesus' campaigns in villages in Galilee and beyond (Mark 10:2-45) constitute a covenant renewal parallel to the covenant speech in Q.[12] It has long been recognized that Jesus' teachings in these dialogues bring together traditional materials dealing with social concerns that invite comparisons to other social movements such as the Qumran community, especially in its Community Rule, which was clearly a renewed covenant.[13] Moreover, what have been called "statements of holy law," general statements of law or principle on issues of central importance to the community, figure prominently at several points in this sequence of teachings (Mark 10:10-11, 14, 29-30, 43-44).[14] In the dialogues of Mark 10 Jesus delivers these general principles on the four successive issues of marriage, social status, economic relations, and political relations.

The first dialogue (Mark 10:2-12) deals with the integrity of marriage and the family, a key issue for any traditional peasant society, insofar as the family was the basic unit of production and reproduction. Two out of six of the principles of social relations in the Mosaic covenant are devoted directly to this central concern: "You shall not commit adultery" and "Honor your father and mother." The question that the Pharisees put to test Jesus immediately signals the introduction of a covenantal-legal issue: "Is it lawful for a man to divorce his wife?" For the benefit of his Galilean and other peasant audiences, Jesus fires back at them that the Mosaic commandment they cite from their "great tradition" was given "to stimulate [their] hardness of heart." Contrary to the Christian stereotype of the Pharisees as rigorists on the Law, their contemporary opponents who wrote the Dead Sea Scrolls labeled them "smooth interpreters" because they were lax "liberal" accommodators of the law to their own interests. Jesus' accusation that they are "hard of heart," therefore, must refer to the ulterior motives and results of their permissive attitude toward divorce (and remarriage)—perhaps to the economic plight of the wives who would be so summarily "put away" with a mere "certificate of dismissal."

Jesus' own concern must have to do with the disintegration of marriage and family units under the pressures of Roman rule discussed above. In contrast with those Pharisees who permissively allowed the elite (such as Herod Antipas himself) to divorce and remarry as a device to consolidate their control of land and other resources, Jesus insists on the strict maintenance of the marriage bond. The principle he enunciates in 10:11-12 reinforced marriage and the household with strict prohibition of divorce for the purpose of remarriage. The marriage and family Jesus was reinforcing with this principle were still patriarchal. We can hardly claim that Jesus had anticipated modern concerns for the equality of women. Yet the formulation of the principle in addresses to both men and women is striking in the context of a patriarchal society and tradition.

It may be difficult for modern hearers to understand how the next, brief dialogue focused on "children" that keys it to a covenant context (Mark 10:13-16). Given the historical context of Markan material in the circumstances of Roman Palestine-Syria, however, at least two possibilities emerge from the dialogue contents. There may have been an unusual number of orphans created by the historical circumstances. Or Jesus may be using children as paradigms of status in the renewed covenantal community. Some modern interpreters of this episode tend to sentimentalize children, forgetting that "childhood" is a creation of the modern Western middle class. In ancient Palestine, as in most traditional societies, children were, in effect, the persons with the lowest status in the village community. That "the kingdom of God belongs" to *children* pointedly reminds the hearers that the renewed village communities are for humble ordinary people, in contrast to people of standing, wealth, and power—as picked up in the following dialogues.

Jesus gives greatest attention to economic relations in the communities undergoing renewal in response to the presence/imminence of the kingdom of God. What is often separated into three paragraphs in English Bibles (Mark 10:17-22, 23-27, 28-31) should all be read together as a statement of egalitarian covenantal economics. Because of the American emphasis on political and not economic rights and separation of economics and religion, American biblical interpreters tend to miss the importance of economics in the Mosaic covenant. All of the six social commandments either focus on or include concern for people's economic rights: "You shall not covet," "you shall not steal," and "you shall not bear false witness" all protect people's economic resources and rights in the interaction of community members. The other three, no murder, no adultery, and honoring father and mother, include economic aspects.

This becomes evident quickly in Jesus' response to the man who asks how he can inherit eternal life—not exactly the kind of question that a hungry, marginal peasant would ask. Jesus immediately recites the covenant commandments. It is not clear whether his inclusion of "You shall not defraud" is a pointed addition in a list that happens to omit "You shall not covet," or a pointed substitution for the latter that gives it a telling concrete application. Coveting someone else's goods would lead the coveter to defraud a vulnerable person desperate for wage labor or for a loan to feed his children (cf. Deut 24:14-15). The man's insistence that he has kept these commandments is obviously phony. Of course he cannot respond to Jesus' command to sell his goods and give to the poor because he not only has great possessions but is deeply attached to them. The only way someone became wealthy in ancient Israelite society was by taking advantage of others who were vulnerable, for example, defrauding others by charging interest on loans, which was forbidden in covenant law, and gaining control of others' possessions (labor, fields, households). This episode thus provides a negative example of a man who has gained wealth by defrauding others, by breaking the covenant commandments.

With this negative example in mind, Jesus reflects on its implications in the ensuing dialogue with the uncomprehending disciples (Mark 10:23-27). From the particular case of how extremely difficult it will be for the rich to enter the kingdom of God (10:23) he moves to the more general situation of anyone (10:24), then back to the rich (10:25). The proverb about the camel going through the eye of the needle, meaning that it is impossible for the wealthy man to enter the kingdom of God, is a piece of peasant humor. As often in biblical materials that derive from popular tradition, so in this episode peasant hostility against their wealthy rulers and exploiters is not even veiled. The criteria for "entering the kingdom" are the simple and straightforward covenantal economic principles. The rich man in the previous dialogue is the negative example of one who, as evidenced in his wealth, has not kept them.[15]

We must listen with peasant ears to Jesus' statement in reply to Peter's self-interested query in the next dialogue:

> Truly I tell you, there is no one who has left house or brothers or sisters or mother or father or children or fields, for my sake and the gospel's, who will not receive a hundredfold now in this age (houses, brothers and sisters, mothers and children, and fields) with persecutions—and in the age to come eternal life. (10:29-31)

This is an astoundingly this-worldly reassurance. The restoration is to occur "now in this age." The clause "and in the age to come eternal life" is a throwaway line that refers back to the unreal question of the rich man with which the economic issue was opened. Only people who have gotten rich by defrauding the poor are interested in "eternal life." Jesus' focus on "in this age" is made all the more real by the addition at the end of "with persecutions." He is not talking about "never-never land." He is talking, with wondrous exaggeration, about the renewal of village life entailed in the presence of the kingdom of God, which is happening in this age in the face of (in spite of) persecutions, before the kingdom of God comes with power (Mark 9:1). Jesus' final "statement of holy law" in this third dialogue completes the instruction in covenant economics with a clear allusion to the covenantal blessings. Observation of egalitarian economic principles, where no one seeks to become wealthy by taking advantage of others' vulnerability, will result in (unheard-of) abundance for all in the community, albeit with no illusions about political realities in the larger world.

The egalitarian politics that Jesus insists upon in the next dialogue (Mark 10:32-45) matches the egalitarian economic dimension of the covenant renewal of Israelite village communities. Continuing their utter incomprehension even after his third announcement that the Jerusalem rulers will condemn him and the Romans execute him, two leading disciples request that Jesus appoint them to the highest positions of power at his right hand and left hand when he comes into his glorious power. They are borrowing an image of imperial rule, as if that is what Jesus' program of the kingdom of God is all about. After reminding them that he is headed to a martyr's death by crucifixion—where those "on his right and on his left" will turn out to be fellow "brigands" similarly executed by the Romans—Jesus enunciates his final principle, on political relations in the renewed covenantal community. He draws a pointed contrast with the "great ones" of the nations, the high and exalted emperors who lord it over them, tyrannically exercising absolute domination. His program was the diametric opposite of such imperial rule. Not only are there no rulers in the renewed peasant society, but its leaders serve others.

In sum, in a series of dialogues at the conclusion of his mission in Galilean and other villages, Mark's Jesus addresses the fundamental issues of community social relations: marriage as the basic bond of family/household, social status and demeanor in the community, provision of economic viability for all households, and egalitarian political leadership. He not only focuses on the basic concerns of the Mosaic covenant, but also grounds his own declaration of legal principles with explicit references to the covenant commandments. Hearers of Mark would have understood clearly that Jesus was building on the Israelite covenantal tradition in this program of reenvisioning and reestablishing a common life of cooperation and egalitarian political-economic relations in community life.

While somewhat different in form, Jesus' covenant renewal speech in Q and his covenant dialogues are closely parallel in referencing traditional covenantal forms and teachings and in their basic concern for cooperative social-economic relations in community life. They constitute strong indications that, besides his actions devoted to alleviating the debilitating effects of Roman imperial rule in Palestine, Jesus was engaged in a mission of rebuilding and revitalizing communities in their fundamental social-economic relations.

In this survey of the constructive aspect of the kingdom of God, it is evident that (1) in the crisis of social disintegration under Roman imperial rule, and (2) drawing on the Israelite tradition of prophetic renewal of the people, particularly renewal of covenantal cooperation and justice, (3) Jesus (4) assumed the role of a prophet like Moses and/or Elijah, founder and renewer of the people, (5) in healing the debilitating effects of Roman imperialism and renewing the covenantal community life of the people. Again in all of these respects Jesus was thoroughly embedded in and understandable in terms of the historical context of Israelite peoples under Roman imperial rule.

JESUS' ALTERNATIVE
TO THE ROMAN IMPERIAL ORDER

In both his actions and teaching Jesus opposed the Roman imperial order and its effects on subject peoples. In prophetic proclamations and demonstrations directly against the imperial order, Jesus announced that both the Roman imperial rulers and their exploitative Herodian and high-priestly clients in Jerusalem stood under God's judgment. His mission in Galilean and other villages focused on healing the debilitating effects of imperial violence and on renewing the esprit de corps and cooperative spirit in communities disintegrating under the impact of the imperial order. This mission presents a stark contrast with the Roman imperial order.

The Roman elite assumed that since they possessed the power, they could use it to subject other peoples of the world and to extract resources from them. Peoples who dared oppose the Roman imperial order were simply terrorized with intimidating military violence. Imperial conquests left villages devastated, families disrupted, and survivors traumatized. Intensification of economic exploitation under multiple layers of rulers brought subject peoples under the sort of economic pressures that disintegrated their traditional way of life, especially the fundamental social forms of family and village community. The imposition of Roman imperial order in areas such as the ancient Middle East thus entailed not only military devastation and economic oppression, but the relentless undermining of the subject peoples' traditional culture and social structure.

Jesus launched a mission not only to heal the debilitating effects of Roman military violence and economic exploitation, but also to revitalize and rebuild the people's cultural spirit and communal vitality. In healing various forms of social paralysis, he also released life forces previously turned inward in self-blame. In these manifestations of God's action for the people, and in his offering the kingdom of God to the poor, hungry, and despairing people, Jesus instilled hope in a seemingly hopeless situation. The key to the emergence of a movement from Jesus' mission, however, was his renewal of covenantal community, calling the people to common cooperative action to arrest the disintegration of their communities and to revitalize their cooperation and mutual support.

Jesus found not only inspiring "scripts" of resistance to oppressive foreign rule but also principles of cooperative, nonhierarchical common life in Israelite tradition. On the basis of Israelite tradition, Jesus apparently assumed that God had given families and tribes ancestral land to which they had an inalienable right as the basis for their livelihood. In the Israelite covenantal tradition he found a deep reservoir of teachings designed to keep the families economically and socially viable as constituent members of village communities by maintaining egalitarian social-economic relations.

Appealing to and adapting these traditional values and principles of just and cooperative political-economic relations, Jesus called people to take control of their lives in a social revolution. Because God was acting on their behalf, in judgment and deliverance, they could now take action themselves to check divisive behavior and to (re)establish cooperation. Instead of blaming each other for the poverty that plagued them all, they could come to each other's aid in a restoration of mutual assistance. Instead of suspicion and rancor, they could rekindle a spirit of solidarity. Far from imitating the exploitative practices of the wealthy, taking advantage of others' poverty and desperation to defraud their neighbors, they should renew commitment to covenantal principles of justice in the confidence that God's restorative action was imminent. Instead of imitating the imperial patterns in which "great ones" wielded power over others, those who would provide leadership must become servants of others.

The renewed covenantal community that Jesus advocated and enacted also forms a striking contrast with frequent modern interpretation of his teachings. In the context of covenant renewal, "love" refers not to a feeling or an attitude, but to concrete economic practices in village community, such as canceling debts and generous mutual sharing of resources. In Jesus' program, and the underlying Mosaic covenantal tradition, there is far less of a sense of or emphasis on private property and far more of a sense of commonality in claims on and uses of economic resources than in modern capitalist society. Ironic as it may seem, moreover, this lack of a sense of private property goes together with a commitment to everyone having fundamental economic rights, the right to subsistence living. "Loving" or honoring one another's economic rights, even in circumstances of sharp social conflicts, requires generosity, cooperation, and mutual sharing of resources.

Finally, it is significant to note that it is in circumstances of relative powerlessness vis-à-vis the Roman imperial order that Jesus called for the renewed commitment to covenantal economic and political values and behavior in their communities. But it was precisely in those circumstances of poverty and powerlessness that Jesus and his followers found it essential to struggle to practice those values and principles of justice, cooperation, and solidarity. The imperial order was still in place. But Jesus was calling people to take control of and rebuild their own community life in the confidence that the imperial order stood under God's judgment.

EPILOGUE

Christian Empire and American Empire

> *Empire, learning, and religion have in past ages been traveling from east to west, and this continent is their last western state. . . . Here then is God erecting a stage on which to exhibit the great things of his kingdom.*
>
> —Reverend Thomas Brockaway, 1784

CHRISTIAN EMPIRE

The Empire Strikes Back

Two prophets named Jesus (Yeshua) prophesied doom against Jerusalem in the mid-first century C.E., in very similar fashion. Both were arrested by the high-priestly aristocracy and turned over to the Roman governor for execution. In the case of Yeshua ben Hananiah, who went around delivering his statements to everyone in general and no one in particular (much as modern interpreters picture Jesus of Nazareth), the Roman governor, convinced that the fellow was simply crazy, ordered him beaten and then released him—to continue uttering his prophecies. In the case of Yeshua ben Yoseph, however, the Roman governor ordered him beaten and then had him executed by crucifixion, the torturous death reserved for provincial rebels as well as slaves.

Depoliticized views of Jesus have trouble explaining why Yeshua ben Yoseph was crucified, or their ostensible explanations lack historical credibility. For example, the reductionist view that Jesus was merely in conflict with "Judaism" over the Law or over the Temple runs headlong into the case of Yeshua ben Hananiah. The Roman governor would apparently not have been terribly concerned about such "crazies" who

129

merely uttered prophecies and other sayings. Religious teachers and oracular prophets did not get executed—unless of course they inspired their followers to cut down a Roman eagle from over the gate of the Temple. Nor did (nonviolent) protesters in Jerusalem ordinarily get arrested and killed. Like other rulers of preindustrial capital cities, the high priests and Roman governor in Jerusalem would ordinarily have let a protest, particularly a small-scale outcry, run its course. Only rarely did a client king, such as Archelaus, or a Roman governor, such as Cumanus, panic at the escalation of protest and send out the military.

The Roman governors, however, were quick to dispose of leaders and movements that even gave the appearance of a threat to the imperial order. The military slaughter of the popular prophets and their movements in mid-century by several different governors provides vivid illustrations of the vengeful, terrorizing Roman violence. However it may have happened historically, the execution of Yeshua ben Yoseph as a rebel may well have resulted from a similar concern about the threat he posed to the Roman imperial order.

We have discerned in chapters 4 and 5 that Jesus' program of renewal of (an expanded) Israel over against the Roman client rulers might well have been threatening to the imperial order. If Jesus did carry out a bold demonstration against the Temple in Jerusalem in some way (not necessarily the way Mark portrays it), then that might well have been what led to his arrest. One of the few credible episodes in the Gospel "passion narratives" that appear to be "prophecy historicized" more than "history interpreted" is the Jerusalem rulers' arrest of Jesus by betrayal. That suggests that Jesus and his movement had come to the attention of the Jerusalem priestly rulers and/or the Roman governor, who had determined to destroy him. Since he was not in the open countryside but hidden in and protected by the crowd in the tightly packed city at festival time, they had to proceed surreptitiously at night, outside the city.

Is any greater precision possible regarding the threat he posed? The Gospels offer a number of intriguing parallels with both of the two kinds of popular movements that emerged repeatedly at the time, thus attesting to patterns clearly operative in the society that were rooted in the cultural tradition. The most obvious starting point is surely the charge on which Jesus was crucified, stated in the inscription on the cross: "the king of the Judeans." Was Jesus a "messianic pretender," or did the Jerusalem high priests and/or the Roman governor take him to be another popular king, like Athronges or Judas in 4 B.C.E.? In a very short time after the crucifixion, some of Jesus' followers were referring to him as "Jesus Christ" (i.e., *Christos* being the Greek translation for *mashiah* [*messiah* in Hebrew]). If he was understood as an anointed king so quickly after his execution, perhaps he was already adapting that cultural script in his mission. Certain terms or phrases in some episodes in Mark's Gospel have often been interpreted in this way: the heavenly voice calling him "beloved son" at his baptism, Peter's "confession" ("you are the messiah") at the midpoint of the Gospel, and the "triumphal entry" into Jerusalem. But the "beloved son" could also be a prophet, and Jesus pointedly rejects Peter's "confession." If Jesus is posing as "king" in the entry to Jerusalem, it is clearly as a popular king, judging from the mode of transportation (a peasant's donkey, not an imperial king's war chariot).

If these bits and pieces of "evidence" seem to suggest that Jesus was indeed understood as a popular king by his followers—and/or executed as one by the Romans—then it was only by some of those followers. The speeches in Q give not a hint of Jesus as a popular messiah, and they offer no indication whatever that he was executed by the Romans, for that matter. If anything, Q speeches suggest that he was killed as a prophet, like many prophets before him (Q 11:49-51; 13:34). Jesus is certainly represented in the role of a prophet in the Q speeches generally. Similarly, the Gospel of Mark represents Jesus far more prominently as a Moses- and Elijah-like prophet than as a popular messiah. Given his more consistent and prominent portrayal as a prophet, it seems more likely historically that he was adapting that role from the cultural tradition. But it is also possible that he was adapting both roles or that some followers understood him also as a popular king, albeit not one leading guerrilla war, as had Athronges and Judas.

The Romans, of course, killed both popular messianic and popular prophetic leaders. The main conclusion we can draw from Jesus' execution is based on its method. Given that crucifixion was used mainly for slaves and rebels among subject peoples, the Romans must have understood Jesus to be an insurrectionary of some sort. Then the fact that many of his followers (Paul, etc.) identified strongly with his crucifixion suggests that they identified strongly also with his active opposition to Roman imperial rule. That Jesus was *crucified* by the Roman governor stands as a vivid symbol of his historical relationship with the Roman imperial order. From the Romans' point of view, they had decisively humiliated and terrorized his followers and other Galileans and Judeans with this painful and shameful method of execution of a brazen rebel. From his followers' point of view, his mode of execution symbolized his program of opposition to the imperial order.

The Empire Did Not Have the Last Word

Although the empire had executed Jesus, the empire did not have the last word, by any means, so far as his followers were concerned. This can be seen in several branches of the Jesus movement.

The branch of the movement represented by the Q speeches apparently simply continued in Galilee and beyond. Taking Jesus' death as further confirmation that he was the latest in the long line of Israelite prophets, the people who produced Q continued his program of renewing Israel, partly by continuing to perform his speeches.

The branch of the movement represented by the Gospel of Mark apparently expanded into areas beyond Galilee, including villages subject to Tyre and Caesarea Philippi to the north and villages subject to the cities of the Decapolis to the east. Mark understands Jesus' death as a martyrdom in the service of his own mission, after which Jesus went "ahead" of his followers back to "Galilee" where they were to continue the mission of renewal of an expanded Israel (or Israel plus other peoples) in village communities.[1] The empty tomb at the end of Mark's story and other early materials exhibit how the notion of resurrection, which had for some time been cultivated among scribal circles to symbolize the vindication of their members who had been martyred in resistance to empire (cf. Daniel 7–12), could be adapted in understanding Jesus as a vindicated martyr. That God had vindicated Jesus by resurrection and/or enthronement in heaven was empowering evidence that God was indeed engaged in the broader agenda of judging the empire and restoring the people's independence and common life.

Perhaps the most remarkable evidence that the empire had not had the last word was that Jesus' followers expanded their movement among other subject peoples of the empire. They did this with astounding confidence and drive. From indications in the early chapters of Acts and in Paul's letters it is evident that Peter, Paul, and other "apostles" were convinced that history was running not through Rome but through Israel. Jesus' death and resurrection in fact had become the turning point in history. In those events God had finally begun the fulfillment of the promises given to Abraham that all peoples would receive divine blessings through his seed, now known to be Jesus Christ (Galatians 3). Other peoples as well as Israelites had now become the heirs of the promised blessings. It was now possible therefore for the multiethnic and multicultural communities of these heirs of the promises to form more egalitarian social relations that cut across the fundamental social hierarchies of the imperial order, between Greeks and barbarians (including Jews), between free and slaves, and between male and female (see the pre-Pauline baptismal formula used at entry into the communities in Gal 3:28).

Peter and others apparently thought the fulfillment of the promise to Abraham in Christ meant that other peoples could receive the blessings by joining Israel, by being circumcised. Paul insisted that other peoples could receive the blessings simply by trusting that God had indeed brought about the fulfillment in Jesus' crucifixion and resurrection. With a cadre of other teachers and organizers, Paul set about building communities of the faithful in key cities around the eastern Mediterranean areas of the empire. Paul and his mission are usually understood in heavily Lutheran theological terms. But once we cut through the old theological view, it becomes clearer that Paul was, in effect, building an international anti-imperial movement of an alternative society based in local communities.[2] Moreover, many of the people who joined the communities that Paul and other missionaries founded in the imperial metropolises such as Corinth and Ephesus must have been descendants of slaves and other people whose lives had been disrupted and displaced by the practices of the empire. People who were the products of the imperial disorder created by Rome now formed new communities of an alternative social order, the *ekklesiai* or "assemblies" of the proto-Christian movement.

By escaping from the Lutheran/Protestant theological paradigm according to which Paul's letters have been read for generations, we have recently been able to notice the extent to which much of Paul's key terminology is borrowed from and turned back against imperial discourse. In the Roman imperial world, the "gospel" was the good news of Caesar's having established peace and security for the world. Caesar was the "savior" who had brought "salvation" to the whole world. The peoples of the empire were therefore to have "faith" (*pistis/fides*) in their "lord" the emperor. Moreover, Caesar the lord and savior was to be honored and celebrated by the "assemblies" (*ekklesiai*) of cities such as Philippi, Corinth, and Ephesus. By applying this key imperial language to Jesus Christ, Paul was making him into the alternative or real emperor of the world, the head of an anti-imperial international alternative society.[3] Indeed, Paul insisted to the alternative "assemblies" he helped get started, some of whom were a bit skeptical or uncomprehending, that Christ was imminently to return as Lord and Savior in an imperial-style *parousia* that would apparently terminate the reign of Rome with the full implementation of "the kingdom of God" (see Phil 3:19-21; 1 Cor 15:24-28; 1 Thess 4:14-18). No wonder that Paul had a reputation of having preached in Thessalonica and elsewhere that "there is another emperor named Jesus" and that his assemblies were all "acting contrary to the decrees of Caesar" (Acts 17:7).

Some branches of the movement that began with Jesus and his first followers in Galilee continued to oppose the Roman imperial order and to form what were, in effect, alternative communities that embodied very different values and social relations. Periodically in certain areas a prophetic spirit would reemerge, instilling the drive for nonhierarchical social relations with a burning fervor. In Asia Minor several enclaves of "new prophecy" led by women such as Maximilla, Priscilla, and Quintilla became prominent, as indicated by their notoriety among the critical "church fathers" under the names Priscillians and Quintillians.[4] In areas to the east of Palestine, the Christian movement provided a vehicle for the long-suppressed anti-imperial passions of subjected indigenous Middle Eastern peoples.[5]

The legacy of Jesus and his first followers thus included an expanding and periodically revived movement of opposition to the Roman Empire. Moreover, the communities of the movement constituted alternative values, social relations, and, to a degree, an alternative society to the Roman imperial order. To use an old cliché, they were "*in* but not *of*" the empire. The empire had indeed killed Jesus, but his crucifixion became a symbol of opposition to the empire and an inspiration for many to persist in their desire to sustain an alternative society.

Or Did It . . . ?

What became the orthodox forms of "Christianity," however, resulted from compromise and accommodation to the imperial order. The signs are unmistakable in the New Testament and other early Christian literature. While Paul appears to resist being himself drawn into a patronage relationship in Corinth, he seems to set up a quasi-patronal relationship with himself at the top of a nascent pyramid of power. Paul's successors in the leadership of the assemblies, the ones who wrote the "deutero-Pauline" letters such as Colossians and Ephesians and the later "Pastoral Epistles" (1-2 Timothy and Titus), then shaped what became orthodox Christianity. They accommodated to the basic institution and building block of imperial society, the slaveholding patriarchal family ("slaves obey your masters," "wives obey your husbands"), and established hierarchical authority in monarchical bishops.[6]

The Roman destruction of Jerusalem and the Temple in vengeful retaliation for the audacious Jewish Revolt became an ominous watershed for the nascent Christian movement. While on the one hand claiming to be the true heirs of Israelite history and tradition (supercessionism), leaders of the spin-off movement now known as Christians blamed "the Jews" in their attempt to ward off Roman suspicion of their own communities' subversive tendencies. The two-volume work Luke-Acts in particular, while still representing the Christian movement and communities as an alternative to empire, softens the subversive implications of Jesus' prophetic teachings and explicitly places blame on the Jews for their difficulties, while absolving Roman officials of responsibility. Most significantly the Gospels of Luke and Matthew blame the Jews, or at least the Judean priestly rulers, for the death of Jesus, and present the destruction of the Temple as God's judgment.

The expansion of the Christian churches throughout the Roman Empire made them a significant force in the wider society. After many attempts to check or suppress the movement, the Roman imperial state decided rather to use it. After generations of increasing accommodation to the imperial order, the churches were finally recognized as the official, established religion of the Roman Empire by the emperor Constantine. Both in the eastern empire centered in Constantinople and in the western empire still centered in Rome, orthodox Greek and Latin

Christianity became the religion of empire. The terminology that Paul had borrowed to turn back against the empire was only too easily adaptable in support of the empire. Christ became not the anti-imperial Lord and Savior, but the imperial King who authorized the emperor and the imperial order. One could argue that the emperor, who used to be the divine king, suffered a bit of a demotion in his subordination to Christ, now the eternal divine King. The bishops of the church were able to manage some cultural and moral leverage on imperial rule. Henceforth, however, Christ functioned primarily to authorize the empire and the imperial order. While containing subversive materials, the New Testament finally canonized by the now imperial religion also included corrective materials that supported the imperial order, just as the scriptures comprising the Hebrew Bible (Old Testament), while containing subversive materials, had been produced largely in authorization of the imperially sponsored Judean temple-state.

Whenever subject peoples had access to the Gospels, of course, they could still hear a Jesus who pronounced that the kingdom of God meant judgment of oppressive rulers and promised blessings for the poor and hungry. When some secular clergy in certain areas of medieval Europe translated the Gospel lessons for Sunday into the vernacular, many groups of peasants who heard the Gospel for the first time in language they could understand mounted resistance to their temporal lords. One of the principal sources of inspiration for the more extensive movements of the Wycliffites (Lollards) in England in 1381 and the Hussites in Bohemia around 1400 was a hearing of Gospel stories and speeches of Jesus.

Not surprisingly, the Roman Catholic Church forbade the translation of the Bible into the vernacular. While appealing to the Bible for its authority, on the other hand, the Reformation vitiated its revolutionary potential. Martin Luther made it valid mainly for faith, in the spiritual kingdom of Christ, and virtually inapplicable to the temporal kingdom—and called on the German lords to "slaughter the thieving and murdering hordes of peasants" who dared claim that their ancestral rights were supported by the covenantal law of God. The Anglican divines dutifully produced the King James translation, which provided biblical authority in numerous ways to the nascent imperial designs of the English monarchy in the claiming and settlement of America.

AMERICAN EMPIRE

Americans who identify with the mission of Jesus and who are experiencing an uneasy feeling that they are more analogous to the ancient Romans than to the Middle Eastern peoples among whom Jesus carried out his mission may want to take a second look at American identity as a biblical people and its practice of republican virtue. For those two strands of the early American identity became woven together into an ideology of the United States as the new Israel, God's chosen people with a historic mission, and as the new Rome destined to bring civilization, law, and order to the whole world. Most remarkable are the many ways in which U.S. history resembles and repeats the history of Rome as a republic that built and ruled an empire.[7]

America's Manifest Destiny: The New Rome

The Puritans thought of themselves as persecuted people, like early Israel fleeing tyranny in order to establish a new covenant society. In the heady aftermath of the victorious Revolutionary War, that American self-image escalated into the new Israel solidly established in the sacred promised land, a people chosen by God to bring redemption and righteousness to the world. In establishing their covenant communities in the promised land, the Puritans had no qualms about displacing and destroying the original inhabitants of the land. The "Indians" were heathen savages, dark-skinned servants of Satan. The story of the Israelites' "conquest" of the promised land in the King James Bible authorized the slaughter of "the inhabitants of the land,"[8] while the Psalms declared the messianic responsibility to shatter the heathen "with a rod of iron." Within a few decades after the Revolution, fought under the declaration that "all men are created equal . . . ," the new Israel had killed or expelled virtually all Native Americans from east of the Mississippi, climaxing a historically unprecedented process of ethnic cleansing. And so it proceeded right across the continent. The ancient Roman Republic had gradually taken over all the lands in Italy. But it had incorporated the peoples it conquered, not exterminated them.

The United States as the new Rome was from the beginning conceived as an empire, not just a republic. Some of the "founding fathers" were uneasy about an empire of land accompanied by imperial tyranny and militarism. For a republic of popular sovereignty, however, expansion into a vast empire would be a blessing, a way of avoiding the corruption of republican virtue. Historically, of course, it was the Roman Republic that built the empire in its relentless conquest of the ancient Mediterranean world. Similarly, conceiving of itself in benign terms as extending the realm of law and civilization, the American Republic took over much of the North American continent. Typical of the heady atmosphere and imperial self-confidence in the aftermath of the Revolution is an ode to the rising American glory by David Humphrey, one of George Washington's protégés.

> All former empires rose, the work of guilt,
> On conquest, blood, or usurpation built;
> But we, taught wisdom by their woes and crimes,
> Fraught with their lore, and born to better times;
> Our constitutions form'd on freedom's base,
> Which all the blessings of all lands embrace;
> Embrace humanity's extended cause,
> A world of our empire, for a world of our laws.[9]

Implicit in those lines and explicit in this chapter's epigraph was the double notion that "civilization was always carried forward by a single dominant people and that historical succession was a matter of westward movement."[10] The latter apparently comes from a common ancient scheme of a sequence of empires that moved successively to the west, known mainly from the book of Daniel. Ironically in the original Danielic vision, the last, western empire is the most brutal and oppressive of all, making the subjugated people desperate for God's judgment of arrogant empires and the restoration of the people to their own independent sovereignty. Indeed, during the two centuries prior to the time of Jesus, it was just such visions that enabled Israelites persistently to resist the succession of western empires (see chapter 2).

The leaders of the American Republic, however, in their identity as the latest and perhaps final empire, proceeded to imitate imperial Rome in pursuing their "manifest destiny." In an 1845 statement opposing the war against Mexico in which the United States took over half of Mexico's territory, a former congressman from New York envisaged what for him was a frightening future for an imperial America: "Contemplating this future, we behold all seas covered by our fleets; our garrisons hold the most important stations of commerce; an immense standing army maintains our possessions; our traders have become the richest, our demagogues the most powerful, and our people the most corrupt and flexible in the world."[11] It is difficult to imagine that he could have been any more clairvoyant, given how American history unfolded in the rest of the nineteenth and particularly in the last half of the twentieth century.

Just as the Roman Republic, after taking over Italy, began building an empire around the Mediterranean, so the American Republic extended its empire beyond the North American continent. Pursuing its manifest destiny in a flurry of military adventures in 1898, the United States seized Cuba and Puerto Rico in the Caribbean, and Guam, Wake Island, and Manila in the Pacific. It then fought a long war of colonial subjugation in the Philippines, helped quell the Boxer Rebellion in China, and gained control of territory in Panama to build the canal. The United States thus finally joined the major European powers in carving out a worldwide empire.

The way was prepared and the new phase of American imperialism justified by leading clergy and politicians in convenient concert. Preparing the way in 1885 was the popular tract *Our Country* by Josiah Strong, liberal theologian and strong advocate of both missions abroad and the social gospel at home. Reviving both the new Israel and westward empire themes, Strong argued that God had charged the United States, which "had already achieved the lead in material wealth and population, as well as the highest degree of Anglo-Saxonism and true Christianity," with the task of Christianizing and civilizing the world.[12]

Since European-style imperialism was "alien to American sentiment, thought, and purpose," according to President McKinley, its apologists found euphemisms, such as "empire of peace" and the Jeffersonian "empire of liberty." Following the British lead, the United States was now destined to create a "democratic empire," turning colonialism into a kind of tutelage in self-government—to be granted at some indefinitely future date. Since it was "destined to carry worldwide the principles of Anglo-Saxon peace and justice, liberty and law," it could even be called a "New Imperialism."[13] Anticipating President Woodrow Wilson's "new world order" by two decades and (senior)

George Bush's by nearly nine, an 1898 salute to American power by the Catholic archbishop John Ireland proclaimed "a new order of things." Dissenters such as Senator Pettigrew argued that "manifest destiny is simply the cry of the strong in justification of their plunder of the weak." Yet as even establishment critics of American imperialism such as Senator Henry Cabot Lodge had to admit, the United States had a "record of conquest, colonization, and territorial expansion unequalled by any people in the nineteenth century."[14]

Unrivaled in unabashed articulation of the imperialist position was the progressive young reformer Senator Albert Beveridge of Indiana.

> We shall establish trading-posts throughout the world as distributing points for American products. . . . We shall build a navy to the measure of our greatness. . . . Our institutions will follow our flag on the wings of our commerce. And American law, American order, American civilization and the American flag will plant themselves on shores, hitherto bloody and be-nighted, but, by those agencies of God, henceforth to be beautiful and bright.[15]

By achieving commercial supremacy Americans would become "the sovereign factor in the peace of the world," "the master organizers of the world." Thus "nations shall war no more without the consent of the American Republic"—another uncanny prophecy of the American "manifest destiny." But it would take nearly another century for Americans to impose on the world at large what the Romans had imposed on the Mediterranean world two thousand years earlier.

The Sole Superpower

It was Theodore Roosevelt who really set the tone and dictated the terms of the American empire that would be fully realized in the Pax Americana at the turn of the new millennium. He thought that the vigorous young American nation was on its way to becoming the new Rome, the final incarnation in the movement of imperial civilization. Like his social Darwinist contemporaries—and the patrician architects of the ancient Roman Empire who placed tyrants like Herod the Great in power—he understood that it was possible to move peoples from barbarism to civilization only through the intermediate stage of despotism. For (Christian, Western) civilization to carry out its historic destiny in the domination of an unruly world, therefore, required a certain amount of brutality. One must "harass and smash the insurgents in every way until they are literally beaten into peace."[16] As president he practiced what he preached. In his 1904 Corollary to the Monroe Doctrine he transformed in one stroke what had been a warning to keep European powers out of Latin America into an assertion of the United States' intervention with an "exercise of an international police power" against any lapse from civilized behavior in the hemisphere. Roosevelt had thus set the policy and tone in which the U.S. government (often through the CIA) acted later in the century to overthrow elected governments in other countries: for example, in Guatemala and Iran under Eisenhower, and in Chile under Nixon, and to wage war (Desert Storm) against Iraq under George H. W. Bush and, as this book goes to press, possibly again under George W. Bush.

After two decades of relative isolation following the First World War, the United States became the dominant actor on the world stage as a result of the Second World War. Thus began the unprecedented American military mobilization and the deployment of U.S. military forces around the world that has been sustained ever since. In its rise to power in World War II, the United States again resembled Rome in at least one highly significant way. Just as Rome destroyed whole cities such as Carthage and Corinth in its rise as a world power, so the United States wrought awful devastation, only on a much more massive scale. As the only world power to have used atomic weapons, the United States destroyed Hiroshima and Nagasaki to bring World War II to an end more quickly. One suspects that this ability to wreak such devastation on an "enemy" people is rooted partly in the Orientalism and racism that often accompanies imperialism, manifest from the outset of "American" history in the treatment of Native Americans and the enslavement of Africans. Interestingly enough, it is precisely the academic "experts" and the policymakers in the State Department that they train, along with the national press, who articulate the standardized view of Asian, African, and Middle Eastern peoples as stagnant, irrational, and violent, therefore requiring violent treatment.[17] Here again Americans follow in the well-worn path of Western European Orientalism and the ancient Romans, who viewed the Judean and other peoples they conquered and ruled as brutish and violent, "born slaves," who needed to be ruled by a superior civilized people.

The exhaustion of the Western European powers and the ensuing loss of their empires left the United States as the principal remaining superpower. Feeling threatened in the extreme by the "godless communism" and imperial designs of the Soviet Union, the United States organized the "Free World" under its own leadership in networks of military alliances. The cold war "containment" of the Soviet Union enabled the principal remaining superpower to expand its power on a global scale, moving into areas previously controlled by European powers, such as Southeast Asia and the Middle East. Like the ancient Roman Republic, the American Republic in the decades following World War II spread its imperial power and control "overseas" in a series of wars and treaties with weaker peoples. Just as Rome controlled subject peoples through client rulers such as the Herodian kings and the Jerusalem high priests, so the United States controlled many countries through military dictators such as Marcos in the Philippines, the Somozas in Nicaragua, the Shah in Iran, and the repressive Saudi regime in Arabia. As the Romans brought massive military force to bear on rebellions by subject peoples, so the U.S. government, in its struggle against "communism," fought undeclared wars with massive force, most destructively in Vietnam, or armed and trained local military regimes, as in El Salvador, to suppress peasant insurgencies. Just as Roman devastation and killing among peoples such as the Galileans and Judeans left behind a collective social and personal trauma, so the U.S. military devastation of the Vietnamese and the U.S.–trained Salvadoran military's treatment of Salvadoran campesinos (like the Soviet treatment of the Afghanis) left collective trauma in its wake. With the arms race, including the massive military buildup under President Reagan in the 1980s, the "military-industrial complex" about which President Eisenhower warned in the late 1950s became even more entrenched and powerful, devoted to and dependent on continual growth, as well as a continual threat that justified its inordinate power.

Especially striking to people from outside the United States is how fanatically religious American imperialism can be. The ideology developed to justify the cold war and arms race against the Soviets drew upon but went far beyond the new Israel's divine commission to redeem the world and the new Rome as the last great civilizing empire. Cold war ideology became a full-blown cosmic dualism articulated in Manichaean and Judeo-Christian apocalyptic terms of absolute Good versus absolute Evil, the divinely blessed United States versus godless Communism, the Free World versus the Evil Empire. Not only the militarized economic system but the Manichaean ideological system that fueled it became self-perpetuating in American politics. When the United States "won" the cold war and the threat of "godless Communism" disappeared, other threats had to be found against which America could wage war: drugs, Saddam Hussein, and the new "Axis of Evil" projected by George W. Bush. Such an ideology, of course, appears to be self-perpetuating in another way as well, insofar as the other side comes to view the United States as an evil, satanic empire that aims to destroy it.

Transformation of American Empire: The New World Disorder

The United States also spearheaded schemes of international economic controls, in the World Bank and the International Monetary Fund, by which it established its hegemony over the capitalist world and through the latter over the "developing" world. Parallel to the way in which the Romans laid subject peoples under "tribute," forcing them to become economically more productive in order to generate the payments, so the United States pressed a program of "development" and "modernization" on its client states as a way of expanding the global capitalist system. In fact, just as Herod was the Roman emperor Augustus's favorite client king (who sponsored massive building projects), so the Shah of Iran was the model U.S.–sponsored ruler of a Middle Eastern country, forcing "development" programs on his people—except that the American-sponsored Shah was far less sensitive to the traditional culture, institutions, and leadership of his people than was Herod.

As it turns out, schemes of "development" have proven to be effective instruments in draining resources from the Third to the First World, principally the United States. Just as the ancient Roman imperial elite drained subjugated countries of resources to supply "bread and circus" for the masses in Rome, so giant U.S.–based conglomerate corporations drain subordinated countries of resources such as oil and raw materials, and nowadays especially cheap labor, to supply goods to the United States and other prosperous "developed" countries. Cheap gas for SUVs, the fruits of agribusiness, and a plentiful supply of other consumer goods, of course, ensure popular support for imperialism in the United States today, just as comparable goods did earlier in Rome. Of course, the proportion of goods consumed by ancient Rome never even approached the 75 percent of the world's resources currently being consumed by Americans.

The growth and power of huge transnational corporations made possible by the American-sponsored new global economic order started at Bretton Woods points to the major difference between ancient Roman and modern American imperialism: their different forms of "globalization," that is, the differing ways that domination and exploitation are institutionally structured in the imperial power relations. Roman "globalization" was political. Military conquest made possible the economic exploitation that was low-level by modern standards. Modern American imperial power is primarily economic, structured by the capitalist system that has long since transcended American national borders and become global. The huge concentrations of capital wielded by gargantuan transnational corporations, which dwarf the GNP of even intermediate-sized countries, can virtually dictate economic affairs according to the "needs" of global capital (never mind the welfare of the people). There is a certain resemblance between the patronage pyramids that structured economic relations in the Roman Empire and the corporate pyramids of conglomerate multinational corporations. But the scale of the former was nothing compared to the determinative power of the latter. Indeed, the multinational corporations are so powerful that even the U.S. government has little leverage on them. The power relations between government and economics have been reversed, not just as a result of deregulation. Governments now often do the bidding of huge corporations. The globalized economic power of capital now determines political relations. The American empire that has reached the pinnacle of power since World War II has become transformed by its own globalization. The empire now belongs to global capitalism, with the U.S. government and its military as the enforcer.[18] Of course, while increasingly decentered, global capital and its enabling instruments (such as the IMF and World Bank) are still heavily based in the United States, and the culture it sells to the world is predominantly American. Those who selected the targets of the September 11, 2001, terror attacks had an acute sense of symbolism as well as of the real center of imperial power: the World Trade Center and the United States Pentagon.

Recent Resistance

It may also be significant to note that at least some of the most adamant resistance to American imperialism is analogous to some of the ancient Judean and Galilean movements that stood firmly against Roman imperial rule. Perhaps most parallel and similar to the Judean-Galilean peasant movements and revolts were the peasant movements and revolts in Nicaragua and El Salvador in the 1970s and 1980s. Like the popular messianic movements at the time Jesus was born, the Sandinistas achieved independence from the empire for a few years, before the United States wore them down by organizing the Contras and undermining the Nicaraguan economy. In these and other peasant movements in Latin America, one of the factors that generated resistance was newly gained access to biblical stories of liberation, which had been a significant factor in ancient Israelite movements against Roman rule. Like the Lollards/Wycliffites, Hussites, and other medieval European peasants who could suddenly hear and understand biblical stories of the exodus and Jesus' healing and preaching, Salvadoran and other campesinos were catalyzed to take charge of their lives, form base communities, and take action against U.S.–backed rulers by hearing Jesus' "good news" through the "delegates of the Word."[19]

More significant currently for the new world (dis)order are the Islamic resistance movements in the Middle East that bear a strong resemblance to ancient Judean groups. Just as ancient Galileans' and Judeans' traditional way of life was deeply rooted in Israelite culture, including the covenant and covenantal law mediated by the prophet Moses, so Middle Eastern peoples' ways of life are deeply informed by Islamic tradition, including the teaching of the prophet Muhammad in the Qur'an and behind that, the teachings of the previous prophets, Moses and Jesus. In both cases it is impossible to separate the religious from the political-economic dimensions of the cultural tradition and the traditional way of life. In both cases also, the forcible imposition of Western imperial power, political control, and cultural forms evoked strong resistance.

The Iranian revolution against the Shah and American imperialism in 1979 bears some striking resemblances to the ancient Judean Fourth Philosophy and the revolt of the Jerusalemites against the high-priestly regime and Roman imperial rule in 66.[20] Leadership was provided by some of the mullahs or ulama, who in Iranian Shiite Islam are somewhat analogous to the ancient Judean Pharisees and other scribal teachers. The Ayatollah Khomeini and other Shiite "clergy" preached a revival of solidarity among the people in exclusive loyalty to God, much as Judas the teacher and Saddok the Pharisee had in ancient Judea. That solidarity and exclusive loyalty meant refusal to accept the U.S.–sponsored development programs of the Shah, just as it had meant refusal to pay the tribute to Caesar. The Iranian peasantry were not heavily involved in 1979 and virtually no insurgent violence was involved, in contrast to the Judean revolt of 66. But leadership by Shiite clergy and intellectuals and repeated mass demonstrations by the people in Tehran overthrew the Shah and expelled the American corporations and their officers, just as leadership by teachers and ordinary priests and rallies by the Jerusalem populace sent the high-priestly families into hiding or exile and drove out the Roman garrison.

In what is surely the most unsettling modern analogy to ancient Judean resistance to the ancient Roman imperial order, the terrorism carried out by certain Middle Eastern groups parallels the acts of terrorism by the Sicarii in ancient Jerusalem. In both cases, apparently, educated people who were aware of how the imperial power had eliminated virtually all other means of protest and despaired at the overwhelming power arrayed against them, felt they had no alternative to acts of terror to get the attention of their rulers.[21] It is significant that in all of these ancient and modern cases, the empire, in effect, generated the resistance by its severe economic oppression and/or its intransigent political repression.

As the scale of the American/global capitalist empire has grown exponentially over that of the Roman Empire, however, so the scale of modern terrorist groups has grown, from the more local operations of the Jewish Irgun zwai Leumi in the 1940s and EOKA on Cyprus in the 1950s to the international activities of Al-Qaeda in the 1990s. Whereas modern Jewish and Cypriot terrorists still struck at imperial targets within their own territory, just as the ancient Judean Sicarii struck at their own high priests as symbolic representatives of Roman rule, terror has now struck at the metropolitan center of the empire. The disorder created by empire has struck back. The American imperial regime, like the Roman imperial forces before it incapable of self-criticism and compromise, is now itself striking back with relentless and systematic military action rather than diplomatic negotiation.

Jesus and the American Empire

This survey of the historical rise of the American empire, its many similarities to Roman imperialism, and its self-understanding as the new Rome suggests that the United States has indeed developed an ambiguous identity. Both in the period of settlement and in the Revolutionary War, the colonists and rebels understood themselves as a biblical people, the new Israel achieving liberation from political and religious tyranny and establishing a new democratic covenant. In the excitement of independence, however, political leaders reached for a more grandiose sense of what they were about. The new nation was a new Rome, practicing republican virtue. They soon pretended, however, that building an empire would not corrupt that virtue. Indeed, already in the 1780s clergy as well as politicians understood the newly independent nation as the final incarnation in the glorious succession of world empires that had found its final place in its steady westward movement, as indicated in the epigraph above. Despite the hesitation of some, the American Republic like the Roman Republic proceeded to build an empire, practicing the same brutality against the people it conquered.

The more we learn about the effects not only of ancient Roman imperialism but of modern American imperialism, however, the more uncomfortable we feel about our imperial identity. Film footage on the evening news from the American war on the Vietnamese and pictures in the Catholic press of priests, nuns, and peasants killed by death squads trained by the U.S. military sowed doubts in the hearts of many. American imperialism, however, has not subsided but gained strength as it transformed into global capitalism with the American government and military ready to enforce the new world order.

The intensely religious dimension of American imperialism owes much to the other early strand in the American identity. In the early Puritan settlements in New England there was very little separation between the community as covenant and the church as covenant, patterned hand in glove after God's covenant with Israel. In the new covenant of the U.S. Constitution, however, church was explicitly, institutionally separated from state. The nation, however, more than the churches, emerged as the new Israel. The United States, more than its churches, was the people chosen by God to redeem the world. As this strand of the United States' identity became intertwined with the United States as the new Rome—like the old Rome, bringing salvation and civilization to the world it conquered—it injected an intense religious quality into American "manifest destiny." This religious dimension of American imperial nationalism operates all the more effectively because it is defined and understood as secular in the official American liberal ideology, and therefore not separated off into its own institutional expression, as are officially defined "religions" such as Christianities, Judaisms, Islams, and Buddhisms.

As the United States itself, having co-opted God to bless it, became an object of devotion in the American civil religion, as it assumed the messianic mission of saving the world, the churches and other religious institutions became ever more marginalized. With separation of church and state, it was obvious that Jesus himself had taught the separation of religion and politics, render to God and render to Caesar. With notable exceptions of activist reform movements, such as women's suffrage, the social gospel, and civil rights, the churches have gradually acquiesced in their own marginalization. On the defensive even more as science became the guide of societal life in the twentieth century, churches settled into their confinement to the religious sphere.

Despite the role that the Bible, especially the Mosaic covenant, had played in the formation of the American political order, the churches and theological schools accepted its redefinition as (merely) religious. After all, Jesus himself had established the clear separation of religion and politics: render to God what is God's and to Caesar what is Caesar's. The result, as noted in the introduction, is that Jesus and the Gospels, like the rest of the Bible, are assumed to be religious, separated from the real-world life of politics and economics. Even in American liberal theology, Jesus was constructed as (merely) a religious-ethical teacher, a picture that recent treatments update in terms of a culture critic or an advocate of a radical individual lifestyle. Such a Jesus may serve well in religiously informed formation of individual character. But conveniently for the "secular" pursuit of empire it leaves unchallenged the pursuit of the American manifest destiny as the new Rome by an imperial presidency and global corporations.

By contrast to the depoliticized Jesus of American imperial culture, among many peoples subjected to the American empire Jesus has had direct political relevance and impact. Surely a principal reason that people such as Central American campesinos readily identified with and took action in response to hearing Gospel stories and speeches is the similarity of their own life circumstances to those of Jesus as represented in the Gospels. People whose life circumstances are more analogous to the ancient Roman patricians or the Roman plebs who enjoyed the "bread and circus" lifestyle, on the other hand, may understandably find it difficult to "relate" directly to Jesus' pronouncements and practices. Yet especially in the aftermath of 9-11-01 those living in the imperial metropolis who identify with Jesus and the Gospels may well be questioning how they understand and appropriate this part of their cultural, scriptural heritage. It should be possible to cut critically through the questionable standard depoliticizing assumptions and approaches in order to listen afresh, with antennae attuned to imperial power relations, to the Gospel representations of a prophetic political leader of subject people. In the Jesus movements, some of those subject people took collective action to retake control of their lives under the conditions of the new world disorder that Rome had imposed.

It should be possible also, with antennae attuned to imperial power relations, to discern more critically our own situation and roles in the current new world disorder established by the combination of American political power and the power of global capitalism. What implications Jesus and the Gospels might have for Americans who identify with this aspect of their cultural heritage, however, will become evident only through the collective deliberations and actions of communities located inside the society now at the apex of the new imperial disorder.

ABBREVIATIONS

Ancient Sources

1QM	War Scroll (*Milhamah*)
1QS	Community Rule (*Serek ha-Yahad*)
4QFlor	Florilegium (4Q174)
11QT	Temple Scroll (11Q19)
Agr.	Tacitus, *Agricola*
Ann.	Tacitus, *Annales* (Annals)
Ant.	Josephus, *Antiquities of the Judeans*
Ap.	Josephus, *Against Apion*
Bell Gall	Julius Caesar, *Bellum Gallicum* (Gaellic Wars)
Carm.	Horace, *Carmen* (Odes)
Ep.	Pliny the Younger, *Epistulae* (Letters)
Leg. Man	Cicero, *Pro Lege Manilia* (Law of Manilius)
Mith.	Appian, *Mithradateios* (Mithradates Dynasty)
Nat. Hist.	Pliny the Elder, *Naturalis historia* (Natural History)
OGIS	*Orientis graeci inscriptiones selectae.* Edited by W. Dittenberger. 2 vols. Leipzig, 1903–1905
Pomp.	Plutarch, *Pompeius* (Pompey)
Ps. Sol.	*Psalms of Solomon*
Q	Sayings Gospel Q
Sat.	Juvenal, *Satirae* (Satires)
Verr.	Cicero, *In Verrem* (On Verres)
War	Josephus, *Judean War*

Modern Sources

ANRW	*Aufstieg und Niedergang der römischen Welt*
BA	*Biblical Archaeologist*
CBQ	*Catholic Biblical Quarterly*
CSSH	*Comparative Studies on Society and History*
HermeneiaSup	Hermeneia: Supplements
HTR	*Harvard Theological Review*
JAAR	*Journal of the American Academy of Religion*
JMH	*Journal of Military History*
JR	*Journal of Religion*
JSJ	*Journal for the Study of Judaism*
JSNT	*Journal for the Study of the New Testament*
JSNTSup	JSNT Supplement Series
JSOTSup	Journal for the Study of the Old Testament Supplement Series
JSP	*Journal for the Study of the Pseudepigrapha*
NTS	*New Testament Studies*
P & P	*Past and Present*
SDSSRL	Studies in the Dead Sea Scrolls and Related Literatures
SemStud	Semeia Studies
SocT	*Society and Theory*
SPNT	Studies in the Personalities of the New Testament
TSAJ	Texte und Studien zum antiken Judentum
VPT	Voices in Performance and Text

NOTES

INTRODUCTION
American Identity and a Depoliticized Jesus

Epigraph: Edward W. Said, *Culture and Imperialism* (New York: Random House, 1993), 318.

1. The origins of America as a new Israel in historical experiences interpreted as a new exodus and new covenant, etc., have been widely discussed in books such as Robert Bellah, *The Broken Covenant* (New York: Seabury, 1975; 2d ed., Chicago: University of Chicago Press, 1992); Reinhold Niebuhr, *The Irony of American History* (New York: Scribner's, 1952); and Ernest Lee Tuveson, *Redeemer Nation* (Chicago: University of Chicago Press, 1967); with more precise historical investigation, for example, in Perry Miller, *Errand into the Wilderness* (New York: Harper & Row, 1956); and Kenneth Lockridge, *A New England Town: The First Hundred Years, Dedham, Massachusetts, 1636–1736* (New York: Norton, 1970).

2. A burgeoning supply of literature reviewing African American appropriation of the Bible, from the time of slavery through the civil rights movement, is now emerging, of which a significant sampling can be found in Cain Hope Felder, ed., *Stony the Road We Trod: African American Biblical Interpretation* (Minneapolis: Fortress Press, 1991); and Vincent Wimbush, ed., *African Americans and the Bible: Sacred Tests and Social Textures* (New York: Continuum, 2000).

3. Robert Bellah's delineations of American civil religion, widely discussed since, were originally published as "Civil Religion in America," *Daedalus* 96 (winter 1967) 1–21.

4. Perhaps the best-known book by Walter Rauschenbusch is *A Theology for the Social Gospel* (New York: Macmillan, 1917).

5. The United States as the new Roman republic, with great opportunity to exercise its "republican virtue," has been explored by Bernard Bailyn, *The Ideological Origins of the American Revolution* (Cambridge: Belknap Press, 1967); and

Forrest McDonald, *Novus Ordo Seclorum: The Intellectual Origins of the Constitu-tion* (Lawrence: University Press of Kansas, 1985); and Anders Stephanson, *Manifest Destiny: American Expansion and the Empire of Right* (New York: Hill and Wang, 1995).

6. The imperial expansion of the United States is described, for example, by Richard W. Van Alstyne, *The Rising American Empire* (New York: Oxford University Press, 1960); V. G. Kiernan, *America: The New Imperialism: From White Set-tlement to World Hegemony* (London: Zed, 1978). Richard Barnet, *The Roots of War* (New York: Atheneum, 1972), compares the United States' assumption that it has the right to use its power to control the world to early Roman imperial prac-tices, as understood by that ancient Roman imperial statesman, Cicero.

7. In characterizing—and perhaps, with apologies, caricaturing—the standard scholarly analysis and interpretation of Jesus and his context as "depoliticized," I am criticizing no interpreters in particular but the whole dominant discourse and prevailing paradigm of New Testament studies in general. Since interpreters are trained, virtually "socialized," in an already standardized conceptual apparatus, one that owes much to the Christian theological "interpretive community" and professional guild to which we are responsible, it becomes difficult to see histori-cal realities in different ways. At key points, of course, I am referring to the highly sophisticated development of standard scholarly approaches by leading scholars associated with the Jesus Seminar, founded by Robert Funk. The hypothesis that Jesus resembled the vagabond Cynic philosophers, which has so intrigued liberal interpreters recently, has been critically examined, for example, by Hans Dieter Betz, "Jesus and the Cynics: Survey and Analysis of a Hypothesis," *JR* 74 (1994) 453–76.

8. Underlying the standard procedural fragmentation of "data" was the pecu-liarly Protestant (individualistic) habit of reading the Bible, esp. the Gospels, in separate verses (as can be seen by opening up a King James Bible).

9. Very recently the political dimension of the Roman imperial context of Jesus and the New Testament are receiving more critical attention. See esp. Richard A. Horsley, *Jesus and the Spiral of Violence: Popular Jewish Resistance in Roman Pales-tine* (San Francisco: Harper & Row, 1987; Minneapolis: Fortress Press, 1993); *idem, Galilee: History, Politics, People* (Valley Forge, Pa.: Trinity Press Interna-tional, 1995); *idem, Hearing the Whole Story: The Politics of Plot in Mark* (Louisville: Westminster John Knox, 1991); *idem,* ed., *Paul and Empire: Religion and Power in Roman Imperial Society* (Harrisburg: Trinity Press International, 1997); Klaus Wengst, *Pax Romana and the Peace of Jesus Christ* (Philadelphia: Fortress Press, 1987); Walter Wink, *Engaging the Powers: Discernment and Resis-*

tance in a World of Domination (Minneapolis: Fortress Press, 1992); and Warren Carter, *Matthew and the Margins* (Maryknoll, N.Y.: Orbis, 2000); *idem, Matthew and Empire* (Harrisburg: Trinity Press International, 2001).

CHAPTER 1
Roman Imperialism: The New World Disorder

1. Fuller discussion of the rise of Rome to domination in Italy and the Western Mediterranean may be found in William V. Harris, *War and Imperialism in Republican Rome, 327–70 B.C.* (Oxford: Oxford University Press, 1979); and John Rich and Graham Shipley, eds., *War and Society in the Roman World* (London: Routledge, 1993).

2. See the detailed treatment of Roman expansion into Greece and other areas of the east in Susan E. Alcock, *Graecia Capta: The Landscapes of Roman Greece* (Cambridge: Cambridge University Press, 1993); and Robert M. Kallet-Marx, *Hegemony to Empire: The Development of the Roman Imperium in the East from 148–62 B.C.* (Berkeley: University of California Press, 1995).

3. Rome's expansion into the eastern Mediterranean is detailed in Kallet-Marx, *Hegemony to Empire*, 291–334; extensive discussion of Rome in the ancient Middle East is available in Fergus Millar, *The Roman Near East 31 B.C.–A.D. 337* (Cambridge: Harvard University Press, 1993.

4. Fuller discussion in Kallett-Marx, *From Hegemony to Empire*, 315–23.

5. Some of the more recent studies of Roman imperialism that paint a more ominous picture than earlier studies of the impact on subject peoples and have influenced the presentation here are Susan P. Mattern, *Rome and the Enemy: Imperial Strategy in the Principate* (Berkeley: University of California Press, 1999); J. E. Lendon, *Empire of Honor* (Oxford: Oxford University Press, 1997); Claude Nicolet, *Space, Geography, and Politics in the Early Roman Empire* (Ann Arbor: University of Michigan Press, 1991); Harris, *War and Imperialism*; Keith Hopkins, *Conquerors and Slaves: Sociological Studies in Roman History* (Cambridge: Cambridge University Press, 1978).

6. A fuller discussion and a rich supply of references are in J. P. V. D. Balsdon, *Romans and Aliens* (Chapel Hill: University of North Carolina Press, 1979), esp. 30–54, 60–70; and Mattern, *Rome and the Enemy*, esp. 66–80. It is striking how ancient Roman attitudes toward the people they subjected resemble attitudes toward other peoples in modern imperial societies (France, Britain, United States); this is examined in the eye-opening study by Edward W. Said, *Orientalism* (New York: Random House, 1978).

7. Fuller discussion in Mattern, *Rome and the Enemy*, esp. 163–64.

8. Further discussion and citations in Mattern, *Rome and the Enemy*, 169; and Nicolet, *Space, Geography, and Politics*, 35–37.

9. Fuller treatment of the Roman imperial administration in Peter Garnsey and Richard Saller, *The Roman Empire: Economy, Society, and Culture* (Berkeley: University of California Press, 1987), chap. 2; and Lendon, *Empire of Honor*, chap. 4.

10. The research and interpretation of the "emperor cult" by Simon R. F. Price, *Rituals and Power: The Roman Imperial Cult in Asia Minor* (Cambridge: Cambridge University Press, 1984), and Paul Zanker, *The Power of Images in the Age of Augustus* (Ann Arbor: University of Michigan Press, 1988), have led to a new appreciation of how important the multifaceted honors to the emperor were in constituting imperial power relations. Selections from their studies are available in Richard A. Horsley, ed. *Paul and Empire: Religion and Power in Roman Imperial Society* (Harrisburg: Trinity Press International, 1997), 47–86.

11. For further discussion see the excerpts by Garnsey and Saller, "Patronal Power Relations," and Richard Gordon, "The Veil of Power," in Horsley, *Paul and Empire*, 96–103 and 126–37.

12. The following is based on Garnsey and Saller, *The Roman Empire*, esp. 83–85, 95–96; and Peter Garnsey, *Famine and Food Supply in The Graeco-Roman world: Responses to Risk and Crisis* (Cambridge: Cambridge University Press, 1988), esp. 231. The classic study is Paul Veyne, *Bread and Circus* (London: Penguin, 1990).

13. A fuller discussion with numerous references is in Mattern, *Rome and the Enemy*, 168–70; Nicolet, *Space, Geography, and Politics*, 29–47; Zanker, *The Power of Images*, 185–92. Erich S. Gruen, *Studies in Greek Culture and Roman Policy* (Berkeley: University of California Press, 1996), 190–94; Andrew Wallace-Hadrill, "The Emperor and His Virtues," *Historia* 30 (1981): 322–23.

14. Mattern, *Rome and the Enemy*, 119. The role of terrorization in Roman imperial policy has been noted before, but its central importance is only recently being recognized. For further discussion see Edward Luttwak, *The Grand Strategy of the Roman Empire From the First Century A.D. to the Third* (Baltimore: Johns Hopkins University Press, 1976), 3–4; E. L. Wheeler, "Methodological Limits and the Mirage of Roman Strategy," *JMH* 57 (1993): 35–36; see also Mattern, *Rome and the Enemy*, 115–22.

15. A suggestive examination is in Martin Hengel, *Crucifixion in the Ancient World and the Folly of the Message of the Cross*, trans. John Bowden (Philadelphia: Fortress Press, 1977).

16. See further Mattern, *Rome and the Enemy*, 117–22.

17. Fuller discussion in Richard A. Horsley, *Galilee: History, Politics, People* (Valley Forge, Pa.: Trinity Press International, 1995), 76–88.

18. Further discussion of the following is in Lendon, *Empire of Honor*; and Mattern, *Rome and the Enemy*, esp. 158, 163.

19. Extensive treatment of Herod is now in Peter Richardson, *Herod: King of the Jews and Friend of the Romans*. SPNT (Minneapolis: Fortress Press, 1999); for a more political-economic and social-structural treatment, see K. C. Hanson and Douglas Oakman, *Palestine in the Time of Jesus: Social Structures and Social Conflicts* (Minneapolis: Fortress Press, 1998). For a good analysis of the unbridgeable gulf that developed between the high-priestly aristocracy and the Judean people see Martin Goodman, *The Ruling Class of Judea: The Origins of the Jewish Revolt against Rome, A.D. 66–70* (Cambridge: Cambridge University Press, 1987)—except that if the hostility was that strong and their dependence on the Romans so clear, they could not possibly have led the great revolt in 66–70. My own more extensive treatment of Roman client rulers in Palestine is most fully sketched in *Galilee*, chaps. 1–7, and *Archaeology, History and Society in Galilee* (Valley Forge, Pa.: Trinity Press International, 1996), chaps. 1–2.

20. Aspects of the face of Roman imperialism presented to the Judean and Galilean people are further cataloged in Warren Carter, *Matthew and Empire: Initial Explorations* (Harrisburg, Pa.: Trinity Press International, 2001), 43–45.

CHAPTER 2
Resistance and Rebellion in Judea and Galilee

1. Stephen L. Dyson, "Native Revolts in the Roman Empire," *Historia* 20 (1971) 239–74; *idem*, "Native Revolt Patterns in the Roman Empire," *ANRW* II.3 (1975) 138–75.

2. Fuller coverage of various revolts can be found in David M. Rhoads, *Israel and Revolution 6–74 C.E.* (Philadelphia: Fortress Press, 1976); Richard A. Horsley, *Jesus and the Spiral of Violence: Popular Jewish Resistance in Roman Palestine* (San Francisco: Harper & Row, 1987; Minneapolis: Fortress Press, 1993), 49–59; and Martin Goodman, *The Ruling Class of Judea* (Cambridge: Cambridge University Press, 1987).

3. For more elaborate discussion see Horsley, *Jesus and the Spiral of Violence*, chap. 1; *idem*, *Sociology and the Jesus Movement* (New York: Crossroad, 1989), chap. 4; *idem*, "High Priests and the Politics of Roman Palestine," *JSJ* 17 (1986) 23–55; K. C. Hanson and Douglas Oakman, *Palestine in the Time of Jesus: Social Structures and Social Conflicts* (Minneapolis: Fortress Press, 1998).

4. Horsley, "High Priests." Goodman, *Ruling Class*, agrees but believes that the high-priestly aristocracy suddenly did an about-face and joined the rebels in 66.

5. Anthony J. Saldarini, *Pharisees, Scribes and Sadducees in Palestinian Society: A Sociological Approach* (Wilmington, Del.: Glazier, 1988); and more recently Patrick Tiller and Richard Horsley, "Sociology of Second Temple Society," in JSOTSup 3: *Studies in Politics, Class, and Material Culture*, ed. P. R. Davies and J. M. Halligan, JSOTSup 340 (Sheffield: Sheffield Academic, 2001).

6. For example, the scribe and sage Jesus ben Sira, author of the book of Ecclesiasticus or Sirach, exhorted his scribal students to protect the poor from exploitation by their patrons, the priestly rulers. This mitigation of the effects of the war of the rich on the poor appears to have arisen from a commitment to the commandments of God. See Tiller and Horsley, "Sociology of Second Temple Society."

7. In early Roman Palestine, however, only a few written copies of books later included in the Bible existed, and those in different versions. See Eugene Ulrich, *The Dead Sea Scrolls and the Origins of the Bible*. SDSSRL (Grand Rapids: Eerdmans, 1999). In the predominantly oral communication context of ancient Judean society, of course, cultural traditions were cultivated by memory and oral recitation; see Catherine Hezser, *Jewish Literacy in Roman Palestine*. TSAJ 81 (Tübingen: Mohr/Siebeck, 2001). Moreover, various forms of what Josephus calls "the laws of the Judeans" were apparently cultivated even in scribal circles.

8. Among the many recent treatments of the Qumran community and the Dead Sea Scrolls, see James C. VanderKam, *The Dead Sea Scrolls Today* (Grand Rapids: Eerdmans, 1994).

9. I have treated the Fourth Philosophy at greater length both in Horsley and John S. Hanson, *Bandits, Prophets, and Messiahs: Popular Movements in the Time of Jesus* (Minneapolis: Winston, 1985; Harrisburg: Trinity Press International, 1998), 190–99, and in Horsley, *Jesus and the Spiral of Violence*, 77–89.

10. Adapted from Hanson's translation in Horsley and Hanson, *Bandits*, 191–92.

11. For example, the scribal *Psalm of Solomon* 17, which appeals for the coming of a scribal messiah, son of David, to restore the freedom of the people on their land, begins and ends with a declaration of the kingship of God. Josephus himself in other contexts explains proudly that the true Judean polity (constitution) given to Moses was a "theocracy" that placed "all sovereignty and authority in the hands of God" and that the God-given "laws" were their "masters" and God their true "ruler" (*Ap*. 2.164–65; *Ant*. 4.223).

12. Josephus couches the same belief of Pharisees in seemingly paradoxical Hellenistic philosophical terms, i.e., that people have free will to act, but that Fate cooperates in every action (*War* 2.163).

13. The principal accounts in Josephus are *War* 2.254–57 and *Ant.* 20.164–65. An important study differentiating them from the Zealots proper is Morton Smith, "Zealots and Sicarii: Their Origins and Relation," *HTR* 64 (1971) 1–19; for a documented critical and comparative treatment that draws on studies of modern terrorist groups, see Richard A. Horsley, "The Sicarii: Ancient Jewish 'Terrorists,'" *JR* 59 (1979) 435–58.

14. Josephus says explicitly that the Sicarii were the continuation of the Fourth Philosophy and that one of their leaders, Menahem, was the son (grandson?) of Judas, one of the two principal leaders of the Fourth Philosophy; see *War* 2.433, 447; 7.253, 255.

15. For example, H. Edward Price Jr., "The Strategy and Tactics of Revolutionary Terrorism," *CSSH* 19 (1977) 52–65; Thomas Perry Thornton, "Terror as a Weapon of Political Agitation," in *Internal War,* ed. Harry Eckstein (New York: Free Press, 1964), 71–99. More recently, with specific reference to the religious factor, see Mark Juergensmeyer, *Terror in the Mind of God* (Berkeley: University of California Press, 2000), esp. chaps. 1 and 7, and the recent studies listed in the notes; and many of the studies in Martha Crenshaw, ed., *Terrorism in Context* (University Park: Pennsylvania State University Press, 1995); and Bruce Hoffman, *Inside Terrorism* (New York: Columbia University Press, 1998).

16. See Juergensmeyer, *Terror in the Mind of God,* 131–33.

17. The following discussion is based on the more elaborate treatment in Horsley, *Jesus and the Spiral of Violence,* 90–99, and the previous studies by E. J. Hobsbawm, *Primitive Rebels* (reprint New York: Norton, 1965); E. P. Thompson, "The Moral Economy of the English Crown in the Eighteenth Century," *P & P* 50 (1971) 76–136; George Rudé, *The Crowd in History* (New York: Wiley, 1964); *idem, The Crowd in the French Revolution* (Oxford: Clarendon, 1959).

18. The following is based on the fuller discussion in Horsley, *Jesus and the Spiral of Violence,* 100–104.

19. Compare the action of the Roman troops' sacrificing to their army standards when they captured the Temple in 70 (Josephus, *War* 7.316), and the discussion in Horsley, *Jesus and the Spiral of Violence,* 103 and n. 36.

20. The following is based on the fuller analysis of the sources in Horsley, *Jesus and the Spiral of Violence,* 110–16.

21. Fuller analysis and documentation of the messianic movements in Richard A. Horsley, "Popular Messianic Movements around the Time of Jesus," *CBQ* 46 (1984) 471–93; and Horsley and Hanson, *Bandits,* chap. 3.

22. The social discipline Simon enforced in his movement once in Jerusalem should be compared with the anticipation of what the messiah, son of David, was anticipated to enact in the scribal *Psalms of Solomon* 17: in the war against

oppressive foreign rulers, the anointed king would "thrust out sinners from the inheritance" and "not suffer unrighteousness to lodge anymore in their midst, thus purging Jerusalem, making it holy as of old" (*Ps. Sol.* 17:26, 29, 33, 36).

23. Fuller analysis and documentation in Richard A. Horsley, "'Like One of the Prophets of Old': Two Types of Popular Prophets at the Time of Jesus," *CBQ* 47 (1985) 435–63; *idem*, "Popular Prophetic Movements at the Time of Jesus, Their Principal Features and Social Origins," *JSNT* 26 (1986) 3–27; and Horsley and Hanson, *Bandits*, chap. 4.

24. The book of Acts mentions both of these movements, but dates Theudas prior to the Fourth Philosophy (5:36) and confuses the Egyptian prophet's movement with the Sicarii (21:38).

25. See especially James C. Scott, *Weapons of the Weak: Everyday Forms of Peasant Resistance* (New Haven: Yale University Press, 1985).

26. James C. Scott, *Domination and the Arts of Resistance* (New Haven: Yale University Press, 1990). The quotations that follow are from pp. xii and 15, respectively.

CHAPTER 3
Toward a Relational Approach to Jesus

Epigraph: Franz Fanon, *The Wretched of the Earth* (New York: Grove, 1968), 106.

1. The work of the Jesus Seminar and particularly that of John Dominic Crossan, in *The Historical Jesus: The Life of a Mediterranean Jewish Peasant* (San Francisco: HarperCollins, 1991), brought the standard approach to the so-called historical Jesus to its "logical"—and most sophisticated—conclusion. (The hypothetical book titles are a nod to the prominence of Crossan's widely read book.) Given the limitations of the standard approach, the most convincing and perhaps most enduring aspects of his treatment come where he departs from his stated method of relying only on sayings, i.e., in dealing with healings and exorcisms.

2. Because they operate with a standardized set of issues and concepts, and precise historical knowledge was not yet available, it has simply not occurred to interpreters of Jesus to investigate, in as precise terms as possible, the particular historical conditions in which Jesus acted (aspect 1) and to investigate, in as precise terms as possible, the cultural tradition out of which he and his followers operated (aspect 2). The essentialist modern scholarly constructs operative in the field, such as "Judaism/Jewish," "Hellenistic," "apocalyptic," or "sapiential," tend to obscure particular circumstances and conflicts. Almost completely ignored have

been the particular social forms of ancient Galilean and Judean society and the social form(s) of the relationship between Jesus and those who responded to him,
which must have been rooted in Israelite cultural tradition.

3. This is being increasingly acknowledged in New Testament interpretation.
See the sketch of political-economic-religious division and relations in Richard A.
Horsley, *Sociology and the Jesus Movement* (New York: Crossroad, 1989), chap. 4;
and K. C. Hanson and Douglas Oakman, *Palestine in the Time of Jesus: Social
Structures and Social Conflicts* (Minneapolis: Fortress Press, 1998).

4. I have attempted to reason critically through the fragmentary evidence toward a tentative historical hypothesis and to explore some of the important implications in *Galilee: History, Politics, People* (Valley Forge, Pa.: Trinity Press
International, 1995), esp. chaps. 1–3 and 6.

5. Fuller discussion in ibid., 147–57, and chap. 11.

6. Fuller discussion in ibid., chap. 6.

7. Explored in ibid., chaps. 8–10.

8. On this aspect and peasant societies generally see the classic study, Eric
Wolf, *Peasants* (Englewood Cliffs, N.J.: Prentice-Hall, 1966).

9. This is much of the purpose of the explorations in Horsley, *Galilee*, chaps.
2–3, 5–7, 8–9; and *idem, Archaeology, History, and Society in Galilee: The Social
Context of Jesus and the Rabbis* (Valley Forge, Pa.: Trinity Press International,
1996), chaps. 2–5. I have attempted to pull together the implications for Jesus and
his movement in Galilee in "Jesus and Galilee: The Contingencies of a Renewal
Movement," in *Galilee through the Centuries: Confluence of Cultures*, ed. Eric M.
Meyers (Winona Lake, Ind.: Eisenbrauns, 1999), 57–74.

10. See esp. James C. Scott, *The Moral Economy of the Peasant* (New Haven:
Yale University Press, 1976).

11. James C. Scott, "Protest and Profanation: Agrarian Revolt and the Little
Tradition," *SocT* 4 (1977) 8.

12. Ibid., 4.

13. Ibid., 19.

14. See further Horsley, *Galilee,* 147–57.

15. See further "Israelite Traditions in Q," chap. 5 in Richard A. Horsley with
Jonathan A. Draper, *Whoever Hears You Hears Me: Prophets, Performance, and
Tradition in Q* (Harrisburg: Trinity Press International, 1999), 94–122.

16. Scott, *Moral Economy.*

17. According to the dominant view in New Testament studies, the Gospel
of Mark was the first Gospel composed, whose narrative was then followed in-
dependently by Matthew and Luke, thus accounting for the parallel material and

sequence in their narratives. Judging from the large quantity of parallel, often verbatim, teachings of Jesus in Matthew and Luke, which is not also in Mark, the two later Gospels must also have used a common, earlier source, called "Q" from the German word *Quelle* = source. For a recent, magisterial review of "Q and the Synoptic Problem," see John S. Kloppenborg Verbin, *Excavating Q: The History and Setting of the Sayings Gospel* (Minneapolis: Fortress Press, 2000), chap. 1.

18. The highly informative and suggestive treatment by Walter Ong, *Orality and Literacy: The Technologizing of the Word* (London: Routledge, 1982), has been criticized for emphasizing this "divide." Most helpful for study of Jesus and the Gospels are the articles by Werner Kelber, "Jesus and Tradition: Words in Time, Words in Space," and John Miles Foley, "Words in Tradition, Words in Text: A Response," in *Orality and Textuality in Early Christian Literature*, ed. Joanna Dewey, *Semeia 65* (1995) 139–68 and 169–80, respectively.

19. Particularly suggestive for study of Gospel materials and the Gospels are John Miles Foley, *Immanent Art: From Structure to Meaning in Traditional Oral Epic* (Bloomington: Indiana University Press, 1991); idem, *The Singer of Tales in Performance*. VPT (Bloomington: Indiana University Press, 1995); and M. A. K. Halliday, *Language as Social Semiotic: The Social Interpretation of Language and Meaning* (Baltimore: University Park Press, 1978). Discussion as it bears on Gospel materials is in Horsley, "Recent Studies of Oral-Derived Literature and Q," and Draper, "Recovering Oral Performance from Written Text in Q," in Horsley and Draper, *Whoever Hears You*, 150–74 and 175–94, respectively.

20. John S. Kloppenborg, *The Formation of Q* (Philadelphia: Fortress Press, 1987), demonstrates that Q is comprised of a set of speeches or discourses, analyzing each one as composed from separate sayings. Alan Kirk, *The Composition of the Sayings Source* (Leiden: Brill, 1998), further explains how Q is comprised not so much of sayings as speeches. Building on Kloppenborg and others, I have demonstrated further that Q must be read/heard as a series of (oral) speeches (and not a collection of sayings) in "Q and Jesus: Assumptions, Approaches, and Analyses," *Semeia* 55 (1991) 175–209; and in *Whoever Hears You*, chap. 4. The International Q Project has critically reconstructed a text of Q (still apparently on the assumption of individual sayings), now available in James M. Robinson, Paul Hoffmann, and John S. Kloppenborg, eds., *The Critical Edition of Q*. HermeneiaSup (Louvain: Peeters; Minneapolis: Fortress Press, 2000). Draper and I have blocked out some of the speeches as orally performed in *Whoever Hears You*. Far from being similar to Q, which presents speeches as communication to a group audience, the *Gospel of Thomas* presents individual sayings or pairs of sayings not as communication but for contemplation.

21. See further the discussion in Horsley and Draper, *Whoever Hears You,* 163, and the references there.

22. See further the discussion in ibid., 167–68, and the references there.

23. Foley, *Singer of Tales,* drawing on the groundbreaking work of Milman Parry and Albert Lord.

24. See further the discussion of contexts in Horsley and Draper, *Whoever Hears You,* chaps. 7–13; and Horsley, *Hearing the Whole Story,* chap. 3.

25. Since Jesus, his followers, and the Synoptic Gospel tradition derived from and articulated a "little" or popular tradition, we cannot use most other Judean or Hellenistic literature, which was from the cultural elites, for direct comparisons. We can only extrapolate by careful circumspect reasoning on the basis of a clear understanding of the different interests represented by the great and little traditions. See further the cautionary comments in Richard A. Horsley, *Jesus and the Spiral of Violence: Popular Jewish Resistance in Roman Palestine* (San Francisco: Harper & Row, 1987; Minneapolis: Fortress Press, 1993), 129–31; *idem,* "Israelite Traditions in Q," in *Whoever Hears You,* chap. 5. Crossan, *Historical Jesus,* adopts the crucial distinction between the "great tradition" and the "little tradition" but still seems to move directly from texts of the former to the contents of the latter (e.g., using *Psalms of Solomon* and Wisdom of Solomon as sources for how Jesus and other peasants, thought).

26. Mark's portrayal of the Pharisees periodically "on the scene" to challenge Jesus, which might seem to contradict this, is actually a good illustration of how the Gospel represents the "hidden transcript." We have no idea whether an actual confrontation with some Pharisees underlies any of these episodes in Mark 2:1— 3:5, 7:1-13; 10:2-9. But Mark's story as communication in Jesus communities portrays Jesus as always besting the Pharisees in debate as he defends their popular tradition against the Pharisees' devious designs. The concept of "hidden transcript" versus the "official transcript" is developed in James C. Scott, *Domination and the Arts of Resistance* (New Haven: Yale University Press, 1990), as discussed at the end of chapter 2.

27. The following overviews of Mark and Q are based, respectively, on Horsley, *Hearing the Whole Story,* chaps. 1, 4, 5, and *idem, Whoever Hears You,* 83–93.

28. References to Q passages are usually given according to their current location in Luke; hence Q 6:40-49 corresponds to Luke 6:40-49, although Matthew's parallel to a particular passage may be closer to the ("original") wording and Luke may have inserted material that was not in Q as he overwrote the Q text.

CHAPTER 4
God's Judgment of the Roman Imperial Order

1. In the late nineteenth century, German biblical scholars constructed this broad synthetic concept by abstracting features from ancient Jewish literature of various genres written over a period of four or five centuries and in a variety of historical circumstances. The literature and its "typical" motifs and symbols, moreover, were read literalistically, without much appreciation of metaphoric and hyperbolic language. Traditional Israelite prophetic portrayals of God's appearance (theophany) to deliver the people or judge their enemies, such as earthquakes and disorder among the heavenly bodies, were read in terms of "the end of the world" and "cosmic catastrophe." How this concept has determined constructions of the historical Jesus is explored at many points in William R. Herzog, *Jesus, Justice, and the Reign of God* (Louisville: Westminster John Knox, 2000).

2. Sometimes God takes a third action, i.e., the vindication of those martyred for their resistance to oppression. Best known is the vindication of the wise teachers in Daniel 12. For fuller discussion see Richard A. Horsley, "The Kingdom of God and the Renewal of Israel," in *Encyclopedia of Apocalypticism*, ed. John J. Collins (New York: Continuum, 1998), 1:304–7.

3. Interestingly enough, in contrast to previous Christian claims about this text, these Jerusalem scribes' vision of the son of David, while articulated in imperial military imagery, was hardly of a violent, "militant" messiah, but of a scribal-scholarly messiah. He would explicitly "not rely on horse and rider and bow, nor collect gold and silver for war," but would "destroy unlawful nations [not with his sword but] with the word of his mouth" (*Ps. Sol.* 17:33, 24).

4. Once we recognize the difference between the "great tradition" and the "little tradition" it seems highly questionable procedure to draw upon documents of the literate elite, such as the *Psalms of Solomon*, as direct sources for what Galilean peasants and artisans such as Jesus and his followers were thinking (cf. John Dominic Crossan, *The Historical Jesus: The Life of a Mediterranean Jewish Peasant* [San Francisco: HarperCollins, 1991], 284–92); and it is even less justified to draw upon Hellenistic Jewish literature such as the Wisdom of Solomon as evidence for Palestinian peasants. We can only reason critically about their respective views from the similarities and differences of their life circumstances determined by Roman rule. Despite their different social locations and interests, their parallel Israelite cultural traditions, combined with their parallel situations of subjection to imperial domination, may have resulted in some parallel attitudes

and views. It is hardly appropriate, moreover, to classify the *Psalms of Solomon* as "apocalyptic" literature.

5. In contrast to the claims of E. P. Sanders, *Jesus and Judaism* (Philadelphia: Fortress Press, 1985), chaps. 2–3. See particularly the Animal Apocalypse and the Apocalypse of Weeks in *1 Enoch* 85–89, 90–91; and the *Testament of Moses*.

6. We are only beginning to discern the contours of the speeches that comprised Q. The prophetic material and parable evident behind Luke 13:28-29, 34–35; and 14:16-24 has been one of the more resistant to scholarly consensus. The proposal by John Kloppenborg (*The Formation of Q* [Philadelphia: Fortress Press, 1987], 223–38) to see here an earlier set of wisdom sayings with later insertion of these prophetic materials and parable is unconvincing. The supposedly primary wisdom speech has no discernible contours and the prophetic materials dominate the ostensible framework in which they were supposedly inserted. It is far more intelligible to see here a long prophetic speech that incorporated at least the prophetic declarations of 13:28-29 and 34-35 along with the parable in 14:16-24 that articulates a parallel message, as explained in Richard A. Horsley with Jonathan A. Draper, *Whoever Hears You Hears Me: Prophets, Performance, and Tradition in Q* (Harrisburg: Trinity Press International, 1999), 279.

7. Text reconstructed following the Matthean wording in preference to Luke's, thus also revising somewhat the International Q Project construction.

8. Horsley, in *Whoever Hears You*, 283; Dale C. Allison, *The Jesus Tradition in Q* (Harrisburg: Trinity Press International, 1997), 178–82.

9. Consideration of the immediate communication context confirms this conclusion. The actual addressees of Q speeches were communities in their common meetings. But this and certain other Q speeches are, within the speech, addressed to an ostensible audience. In the case of Q 13:28-29 the ostensible "you" or "the sons of the kingdom" who are to be excluded from the banquet of the kingdom refer to outsiders, i.e., outsiders who would presume that they would be included with precisely the glorious ancestors Abraham, Isaac, and Jacob. In the minds of unpretentious common people who constituted the real audience, it would have been the arrogant priestly and Herodian aristocracy who were so presumptuous.

10. Note the parallel also with the "woes" against the wealthy that follow the "blessings" on the poor in Q 6:20-23, 24-26.

11. In other cases, mentioned in chapter 2, the Roman governors quickly sent out the military to slaughter such figures as the "Egyptian" prophet who returned to Judea to lead his followers up to the Mount of Olives. Just before the great revolt in 66 the high priests sought to have Jesus son of Hananiah executed, even

though the Roman governor Albinus thought he was merely a maniac (Josephus, *Ant.* 20.169–71; *War* 2.261–63; 6.300–309).

12. I give a fuller argument that this constitutes the dominant plot of Mark's Gospel in *Hearing the Whole Story: The Politics of Plot in Mark's Gospel* (Louisville: Westminster John Knox, 2001), chap. 5.

13. Given the usual assumption that Jesus and "Judaism" belong in the category of religion and not politics and economics, Christian interpreters tend to downplay, depoliticize, or explain away his dramatic confrontation in Jerusalem. Jesus is thus usually seen as (only) a religious reformer, attempting to purify the Jewish religion centered in the Jerusalem Temple. But the Temple, along with its high priesthood, stood at the political-economic as well as religious head of Judean society in general and was an integral institution in the imperial order, from the Temple's origins under the Persians until its destruction by the Romans in 70 C.E. Thus we can hardly continue to pretend that Jesus' demonstration against the Temple was only a religious "cleansing" or merely an attack on the cultic/ritual religion of bloody sacrifice to prepare the way for the more "spiritual" worship of Gentile Christianity. An old device to defuse the implications of the charges that Jesus threatened to destroy and then rebuild the Temple has recently been revived. E. P. Sanders (*Jesus and Judaism*, chaps. 2–3) claims that Jesus presupposed a Jewish eschatological scheme that included a rebuilt Temple. It is virtually impossible, however, to find any Judean texts that include the motif of a rebuilt Temple. We thus need a broader approach and different explanations of what Mark's Jesus meant not only by his purported threat to destroy the Temple but also in the claim that he would build one "not made with hands." While continuing to assume that only religion is involved, Craig A. Evans presents a series of arguments against standard interpretations and important background material for Jesus' prophetic action and speech against the Temple (with extensive references to previous treatments) in "Jesus' Action in the Temple: Cleansing or Portent of Destruction?" *CBQ* 51 (1989) 237–70; *idem*, "Predictions of the Destruction of the Herodian Temple in the Pseudepigrapha, Qumran Scrolls, and Related Texts," *JSP* 10 (1992) 89–147. Richard Bauckham, "Jesus' Demonstration in the Temple," in *Law and Religion: Essays on the Place of the Law in Israel and Early Christianity*, ed. Barnabas Lindars (Cambridge: James Clarke, 1988), 72–89, 171–77, and John R. Donahue, "From Crucified Messiah to Risen Christ: The Trial of Jesus Revisited," in *Jews and Christians Speak about Jesus*, ed. Arthur E. Zannon (Minneapolis: Fortress Press, 1994), 93–121, also present important information on the economic aspects of the Temple system, but without dealing with the fundamental political-economic structure of Roman-dominated Palestine. Several recent

archaeological and architectural studies have made clear that Herod designed the rebuilt Temple to serve simultaneously as a sacred area and a great civic center, following the pattern of the *Kaisareion* devoted to worship of Caesar in Alexandria and official Augustan building programs. See Duane W. Roller, *The Building Program of Herod the Great* (Berkeley: University of California Press, 1998), esp. 216; Lee I. Levine, "Second Temple Jerusalem: A Jewish City in the Greco-Roman Orbit," and Martin Goodman, "The Pilgrimage Economy of Jerusalem in the Second Temple Period," in *Jerusalem: Its Sanctity and Centrality to Judaism, Christianity, and Islam*, ed. Lee I. Levine (New York: Continuum, 1999), 53–68 and 69–76, respectively. Adela Yarbro Collins, "Jesus' Action in Herod's Temple," in *Antiquity and Humanity: Essays on Ancient Religion and Philosophy in Honor of Hans Dieter Betz*, ed. Yarbro Collins and Margaret Mitchell (Tübingen: Mohr/Siebeck, 2001), 45–61, summarizes recent research that explains how the rebuilt Herodian Temple would have been alienating to tradition-minded Jerusalemites. She suggests that Jesus shared the views of the Judean literate elite, such as Ezekiel the priest-prophet and the priestly-scribal dissidents who wrote the Temple Scroll (11QT).

14. The interpretation of Jesus' prophetic action and speech of God's impending judgment of the Temple here depends somewhat on my earlier analysis in *Jesus and the Spiral of Violence: Popular Jewish Resistance in Roman Palestine* (San Francisco: Harper & Row, 1987; Minneapolis: Fortress Press, 1993), 285–300. See also the insightful discussion emphasizing the economic dimension of the Temple and Jesus' prophetic action in William R. Herzog, *Jesus, Justice, and the Reign of God* (Louisville: Westminster John Knox, 2000), esp. 137–43.

15. Bernard Brandon Scott, *Hear Then the Parable* (Minneapolis: Fortress Press, 1989), 237–54, provides an important recent analysis and interpretation, with a clear sketch of the literary context of the parable in each Gospel, including the version in *Gospel of Thomas* 64–65 and a sensitivity to the different performances of the parable.

16. See further Richard A. Horsley, *Galilee: History, Politics, People* (Valley Forge, Pa.: Trinity Press International, 1995), 132–37, 205–21.

17. William R. Herzog, *Parables as Subversive Speech* (Louisville: Westminster John Knox Press, 1994), 98–113, places interpretation of the parable squarely into this historical context.

18. By no means am I suggesting that we revert to trusting Mark's "passion narrative" as a reliable historical report. Episodes in the passion narrative are surely some of the least historically reliable parts of Mark's narrative. Since the motif of "false testimony" in the trial episode is often claimed as good evidence

that Jesus did not take a stance against the Temple, hence was not opposed to the rulers and was politically innocuous, however, we should make every effort to understand Mark's representation here. Far from portraying Jesus as politically innocent and innocuous in the trial episode, Mark ends it with Jesus pointing the high priests and elders to their impending judgment, of which "the son of man coming with the clouds of heaven" was a standing image.

19. Fuller discussion in Horsley, *Jesus and the Spiral of Violence*, 306–17; and Herzog, *Jesus*, 219–32.

20. More extensive analysis in Horsley, *Hearing the Whole Story*, 136–48; *idem*, *Jesus and the Spiral of Violence*, 184–90. In an insightful interpretation Crossan, *Historical Jesus*, 313–20, also sees that demonic possession is an effect of Roman imperialism. Labeling Jesus' exorcisms as magic, however, tends to obscure the political dimension both in demon possession and in the way exorcism is interpreted in the Gospel tradition.

21. Analysis and references in Howard Clark Kee, "The Terminology of Mark's Exorcisms Stories," *NTS*14 (1968) 232–46.

22. In a catalog of references to the symbolic significance of swine in Judeans' dealings with Seleucid and Roman imperial regimes, Warren Carter, *Matthew and the Margins: A Sociopolitical and Religious Reading* (Maryknoll, N.Y.: Orbis, 2000), 212–13, points out that "the pig was a symbol of the Tenth *Fretensis* Legion stationed in Syria, which fought against Jerusalem in the 66–70 war," and that the pig symbolized Rome in later rabbinic literature.

23. More fully explained in Douglas E. Oakman, "Rulers' Houses, Thieves, and Usurpers: The Beelzebul Pericope," *Forum* 4/3 (1988) 109–23.

CHAPTER 5
Covenantal Community and Cooperation

Epigraph: James C. Scott, *Domination and the Arts of Resistance: Hidden Transcripts* (New Haven: Yale University Press, 1990), 199.

1. Highly influential in recent American liberal interpretation of Jesus and the Gospels has been Gerd Theissen, *Sociology of Early Palestinian Christianity*, trans. John Bowden (Philadelphia: Fortress Press, 1978). But this work has been heavily criticized as sociology, history, and textual interpretation by John H. Elliott, "Social-Scientific Criticism of the New Testament and Its Social World: More on Methods and Models," in *Social-Scientific Criticism of the New Testament and Its Social World*, ed. Elliott, *Semeia* 35 (1986) 1–35; Richard A. Horsley, *Sociology and the Jesus Movement* (New York: Crossroad, 1989), chaps. 1–3; Jonathan A. Draper,

"Wandering Charismatics and Scholarly Circularities," in Richard A. Horsley with Jonathan A. Draper, *Whoever Hears You Hears Me: Prophecy, Performance, and Tradition in Q* (Harrisburg: Trinity Press International, 1999), 29–60; and William E. Arnal, *Jesus and the Village Scribes: Galilean Conflicts and the Setting of Q* (Minneapolis: Fortress Press, 2001), chaps. 2–3. The recently fashionable antifamily and antisocial Jesus results from a combination of factors in scholarly approach: isolation of individual sayings, individualistic assumptions, and lack of attention to historical context and cultural tradition and different ways of using language. For example, Luke/Q 14:26 ("hate father and mother," etc.) is taken in isolation and interpreted literally. Although the literary context is not all that clear, this saying belongs at least with the following one about bearing one's cross and following after Jesus and, since it is hyperbole, probably had something to do with commitment, even to the point of martyrdom, which meaning is reinforced by the literary contexts of these and similar sayings in Mark 8:34-38 and Luke 14:25-33.

2. As in Richard A. Horsley, *Jesus and the Spiral of Violence: Popular Jewish Resistance in Roman Palestine* (San Francisco: Harper & Row, 1987; Minneapolis: Fortress Press, 1993), 255–73, in relation to Luke/Q 6:27-36.

3. Werner Kelber, *The Oral and Written Gospel* (Philadelphia: Fortress Press, 1983), chap. 1.

4. We usually think in terms of the east and the west sides of the Sea of Galilee. But because of the contours of the shoreline, Herod Antipas's second capital city, Tiberias, was situated opposite Capernaum and other villages such as Chorazin on a north-south axis.

5. Both Q 9:59-60 and 9:61-62 clearly allude to the story of Elijah calling and commissioning Elisha as his successor, more precisely to saying farewell to/burying one's father. That strongly suggests that Q 9:57-62 was the introduction to Jesus' commissioning and sending out envoys to expand his mission in Q 10:2-16.

6. As we know through the incorporation of popular stories about these northern prophets into the Jerusalem "great tradition" in 1 Kings 17–21 and 2 Kings 1–9. See further the articles in Robert M. Coote, ed., *Elijah and Elisha in Socioliterary Perspective.* SemStud (Atlanta: Scholars Press, 1992).

7. The principles of the Mosaic covenant and its mechanisms such as seventh-year cancellation of debts and release of debt slaves parallel the basic values and functions of other peasantries as studied by James C. Scott, *The Moral Economy of the Peasant* (New Haven: Yale University Press, 1976).

8. Good discussion of the *prosbul* is in Martin Goodman, *The Ruling Class of Judea* (Cambridge: Cambridge University Press, 1987), 57–58.

9. George E. Mendenhall, "Covenant Forms in Israelite Tradition," *BA* 17 (1954) 50–76; Delbert Hillers, *Covenant: The History of a Biblical Idea* (Baltimore: Johns Hopkins University Press, 1969), chap. 3.

10. This can be seen in the very structure of the Community Rule from Qumran (1QS), as laid out by Klaus Baltzer, *The Covenant Formulary*, trans. David E. Green (Philadelphia: Fortress Press, 1971).

11. The following discussion draws from the more extensive discussion in Horsley and Draper, *Whoever Hears You*, 210–25, where the speech is laid out in poetic form appropriate to oral performance.

12. The following discussion draws on the fuller analysis in Richard A. Horsley, *Hearing the Whole Story: The Politics of Plot in Mark's Gospel* (Louisville: Westminster John Knox, 2001), chap. 8.

13. John R. Donahue, *The Theology and Setting of Discipleship in the Gospel of Mark* (Milwaukee: Marquette University Press, 1983), 39; Ernest Best, *Following Jesus: Discipleship in the Gospel of Mark*. JSNTSup 4 (Sheffield: JSOT Press, 1981), 99.

14. Ernst Käsemann, "Sentences of Holy Law in the New Testament," in *New Testament Questions of Today*, trans. W. J. Montague (Philadelphia: Fortress Press, 1969), 66–81.

15. Similar discussion of covenantal economics in Mark, in Ched Myers, *Binding the Strong Man: A Political Reading of Mark's Story of Jesus* (Maryknoll, N.Y.: Orbis, 1988), 271–76.

EPILOGUE
Christian Empire and American Empire

Epigraph: Cited in Anders Stephanson, *Manifest Destiny: American Expansion and the Empire of Right* (New York: Hill & Wang, 1995), 19.

1. Argued in Richard A. Horsley, *Hearing the Whole Story: The Politics of Plot in Mark's Gospel* (Louisville: Westminster John Knox, 2001), chap. 2.

2. Elaborated in Richard A. Horsley, "1 Corinthians: A Case Study of Paul's Assembly in Corinth as an Alternative Society," in *Paul and Empire: Religion and Power in Roman Imperial Society* (Harrisburg: Trinity Press International, 1997), chap. 14.

3. Explored by Dieter Georgi, *Theocracy in Paul's Praxis and Theology*, trans. David E. Green (Minneapolis: Fortress Press, 1991); excerpted in Horsley, *Paul and Empire*, chap. 8.

4. See further Ross Shepard Kraemer, *Her Share of the Blessings: Women's Religions among Pagans, Jews, and Christians in the Greco-Roman World* (New York: Oxford University Press, 1992), chap. 11.

5. See the discussion at points in Fergus Millar, *The Roman Near East, 31 B.C.–A.D. 337* (Cambridge: Harvard University Press, 1993).

6. See Elisabeth Schüssler Fiorenza, *In Memory of Her: A Feminist Theological Reconstruction of Christian Origins* (New York: Crossroad, 1983), esp. chaps. 7–8.

7. Scholars as well as political and religious leaders have long since recognized a number of particular as well as general similarities between modern Western imperialism and Roman imperial rule in the ancient Mediterranean and Middle East, although there may be significant differences even within the parallels. Striking parallels, albeit with a very benign view of empire, were discerned by P. A. Brunt, "Reflections on British and Roman Imperialism," *CSSH* 7 (1964–65) 267–88. We may pick up where he left off. On American imperialism, strongly evident already after the Revolutionary War (on which I was far beyond my own scholarly competence), I am heavily dependent on Anders Stephanson, *Manifest Destiny: American Expansion and the Empire of Right* (New York: Hill and Wang, 1995); Ernest Lee Tuveson, *Redeemer Nation: The Idea of America's Millennial Role* (Chicago: University of Chicago Press, 1968); Conrad Cherry, ed., *God's New Israel: Religious Interpretations of American Destiny*, rev. ed. (Englewood Cliffs, N.J.: Prentice-Hall, 1998); David Armitage, *The Ideological Origins of the British Empire* (Cambridge: Cambridge University Press, 2000); Marc Egnal, *A Mighty Empire: The Origins of the American Revolution* (Ithaca, N.Y.: Cornell University Press, 1988); Ernest R. May, *Imperial Democracy: The Emergence of America as a Great Power* (Chicago: University of Chicago Press, 1991).

8. This phrase translates "those who sit" in various walled cities, often parallel to "kings" or "enthroned ones," hence originally a reference to the rulers of Canaanite city-states, suggesting peasant revolt against the ruling class rather than Israelite genocide against the Canaanites in general. See Norman Gottwald, *The Tribes of Yahweh* (Maryknoll, N.Y.: Orbis, 1981).

9. As quoted in Stephanson, *Manifest Destiny*, 19.

10. Ibid., 18.

11. Cited in ibid., 57.

12. Josiah Strong, *Our Country*, ed. by Jurgen Herbst (Cambridge: Belknap, 1963), cited in Stephanson, *Manifest Destiny*, 80.

13. Stephanson, *Manifest Destiny*, 90.

14. Ibid., 103–4.

15. Albert J. Beveridge, *The Meaning of the Times and Other Speeches* (1908; reprint Freeport, N.Y.: Books for Libraries Press, 1968). Cited in Stephanson, *Manifest Destiny,* 98–99.

16. Stephanson, *Manifest Destiny,* 106.

17. See the suggestive analysis by Edward W. Said, *Orientalism* (New York: Random House, 1978); *idem, Culture and Imperialism* (New York: Random House, 1993), which have generated extensive further analysis and discussion, and a burgeoning bibliography in several academic fields.

18. This transformation has been analyzed in a number of recent books on "globalization." A sophisticated analysis that is simultaneously optimistic and pessimistic can be found in Michael Hardt and Antonio Negri, *Empire* (Cambridge: Harvard University Press, 2000). I have attempted to explore the importance of globalization for New Testament studies in "Subverting Disciplines: The Possibilities and Limitations of Postcolonial Theory for New Testament Studies," in *Festschrift for Elisabeth Schüssler Fiorenza,* ed. Fernando F. Segovia (Maryknoll, N.Y.: Orbis, forthcoming).

19. See Philip Berryman, *The Religious Roots of Rebellion* (Maryknoll, N.Y.: Orbis, 1984); and reflections on analogies with Gospel infancy narratives in Richard A. Horsley, *The Liberation of Christmas* (New York: Crossroad, 1989), chap. 7.

20. I have explored these parallel historical movements in separate sections of "Religion and Other Products of Empire," *JAAR* 71 (2003) forthcoming; excellent analyses of the Iranian revolution and its circumstances are provided by H. E. Chehabi, *Iranian Politics and Religious Nationalism* (Ithaca, N.Y.: Cornell University Press, 1990); and M. Moaddel, *Class Politics and Ideology in the Iranian Revolution* (New York: Columbia University Press, 1993).

21. See again the studies of modern terrorism listed in n. 15 in chapter 2.

INDEX OF ANCIENT SOURCES